The Haynes Used Car Buying Guide

by Mike Stubblefield and John H Haynes

Member of the Guild of Motoring Writers

The Haynes Manual
for evaluating and buying a used car

ABCDE
FGHIJ
KLMNO
PQRST

AUTOMOTIVE PARTS & ACCESSORIES ASSOCIATION MEMBER

Haynes Publishing Group
Sparkford Nr Yeovil
Somerset BA22 7JJ England

Haynes North America, Inc
861 Lawrence Drive
Newbury Park
California 91320 USA

Acknowledgements

We are grateful for the help and cooperation of Neftin Mitsubishi, Thousand Oaks, California and Joey Sportato, Sales manager. Jay Storer also contributed to this project.

A book in the Haynes Automotive Repair Manual Series

Printed in the U.S.A.

ISBN 1 56392 156 1

Library of Congress Catalog Card Number 95-77794

Contents

Chapter 1
Introduction

Chapter 2
The Walk-around Inspection

Chapter 3
The Test Drive

Chapter 4
Detailed Inspection

Chapter 5
The Professional Check

Appendix

Index

# **1** **Introduction**

The concept

Unlike other books, which emphasize how to select a car, where to buy it, how to negotiate with sales people, how to finance a car, etc., the *Haynes Used Car Buying Guide* emphasizes how to INSPECT a car well enough to make a rational decision whether to buy it or keep looking. This process consists of five phases:

1   A fairly quick walk-around inspection (Chapter 2)
2   An engine mechanical inspection (Chapter 3)
3   An interior inspection (Chapter 3)
4   A test drive (Chapter 3)
5   A more thorough inspection of the entire vehicle (Chapter 4)

All five phases are copiously illustrated. Most "how-to-buy-a-used-car" books are bereft of illustrations, save pictures of specific makes and models. In the *Haynes Used Car Buying Guide,* every inspection procedure is illustrated so that the reader knows exactly what to look for, where to find it and what it looks like.

If you still want to buy a vehicle after subjecting it to the exhaustive inspections and tests above, your next step is a second and more thorough inspection by a professional mechanic. During this phase, he will perform:

1   A test drive (Chapter 5)

2   A visual and mechanical inspection, including the underside of the vehicle while it's raised on a hoist (Chapter 5)

Some more mechanically astute readers may opt to do this inspection themselves; some will have a friend who is a professional mechanic do it for them; and some will simply take the vehicle to a reputable professional and pay him for an hour or two of his time. In any case, the *Haynes Used Car Buying Guide* walks you through this inspection with an illustrated check list which explains what the professional mechanic does - or should be doing - when he inspects a used car for a customer.

What kind of car should you buy?

The short answer to this question, of course, is "buy the car you want!" But we're not talking about makes and models here; we're talking about *types* of cars - subcompact, compact, mid-size, luxury car, sports car, sport-coupe, sport utility vehicle, van, truck, etc. Usually, the process of choosing the right vehicle can be reduced to one question: "Does it do what I need it to do?" Here are some general guidelines to think about:

This Suzuki three-door hatchback is a typical subcompact

Subcompacts are also available as four-door sedans such as this Toyota Tercel

Vehicle size
Subcompact

The typical subcompact is a small two-door hatchback (the rear window and perhaps some part of the body below the window are hinged for easy loading and unloading). A few subcompacts are also available as small two- and four-door sedans, and there are even a few convertible models! Most subcompacts have four-cylinder engines; a few use a three-cylinder. They usually have a wheelbase under 100 inches and an overall length of less than 175 inches.

Subcompacts are inexpensive to buy and to operate, but they don't have a lot of room (especially in the back seat area), and they're usually not as zippy as bigger, more powerful models. If you need a back seat big enough for adults, forget it. The back seat in a two-door subcompact is almost impossible to get in and out of. And once you do get in, there's no place to put your legs! But if you're looking for a commuter car capable of transporting one or two people to and from work while delivering truly impressive mileage figures, this is your class!

The interiors of subcompacts can be quite well appointed and comfortable

Compact

Compacts have a little more head and shoulder room, a little more storage space and offer a little less fuel economy than subcompacts. Most compact vehicles are four-door sedans, but are also available as station wagons, coupes, hatchbacks and convertibles. They're typically powered by a four-cylinder engine, although a V6 is an option on an increasing number of these vehicles. Wheelbase is usually around 100 to 105 inches; overall length is about 175 to 185 inches.

The compact Toyota Corolla is typical of most vehicles in its class

The Chrysler LeBaron four-door is a popular compact sedan

Nissan's Altima is a more luxurious compact

Subaru's Legacy is available as a station wagon

The Toyota Camry is available with a four-cylinder or V6 engine

Mid-size

Most mid-size vehicles are four-door sedans; some are two-door coupes, five-door hatchbacks or wagons. Most mid-size models are equipped with a six-cylinder engine, but some entry level vehicles have a four-cylinder and some of the sportier models may have a V8. Their wheelbase is about 105 to 110 inches and overall length is around 185 to 200 inches. Most late model mid-size cars are now as luxurious as a full-size car, but get better mileage and are more entertaining to drive.

The Dodge Diplomat is a typical 1980s mid-size car

Toyota's mid-size Cressida sedan is a rear wheel drive design based on the Supra sports car driveline

The Nissan Maxima is a successful mid-size car

Mercury Marquis mid-size

Mid-size Ford Granada wagon

The roomy full-size V8-powered Mercury Grand Marquis was available as both a sedan and station wagon

Full-size

Full-size cars are usually four-door sedans; some are wagons and two-door models. Most rear-wheel drive (RWD) models use a V8; most front-wheel-drive (FWD) models use a V6. Wheelbase is over 110 inches and overall length is over 195 inches. This is the traditional big American car favored by folks who want a cushy ride.

The ability to tow a trailer is a distinct advantage of a properly equipped full-size domestic car

The Gran Fury was Plymouth's last full-size rear-wheel drive model

The LH series was Chrysler's first all n;ew front-wheel drive full-size entry

Sports car

Cars in this category are two-door two-seaters, often with a convertible top, a peppy engine mated to a stick shift transmission, wide tires, good brakes and firm suspension. Because of a shrinking market, car manufacturers have made later models somewhat more luxurious to widen their appeal. For the average used car buyer, a true sports car is too impractical. They have no back seats for passengers and very little storage space. But for the enthusiast who is willing to pay the increased costs of owning a sports car, the "fun factor" involved makes it well worth it. The power and handling of a top-of-the-line sports cars is truly incredible. If you've never owned a sports car before, and are now ready and willing to reshape your lifestyle around one, discuss the matter of insurance premiums with your insurance agent. Most insurance companies charge a higher premium for a sports car, and you'll probably want to know exactly how much more insurance will cost you going in.

The Toyota Supra turbo is a classic high performance sports car

Nissan 300ZX Turbo sports car

The Toyota MR-2 is a mid-engine design

The Haynes Used Car Buying Guide

The GTI is a popular sportcoupe built by Volkswagen

Sportcoupe

Often based on the chassis of existing models, the sportcoupe is a comfortable and attractive alternative to the outright sports car. They run the gamut from the all-wheel drive turbocharged Eagle Talon and Toyota Celica All Trac to

The performance of the Toyota Celica All-Trac turbo sportcoupe is on par with many sports cars

The Chrysler LeBaron coupe sportcoupe is based on the Dodge Daytona chassis

the Nissan NX, Toyota Paseo, Honda Civic del Sol types (basically rebodied sub compacts). Sportcoupe performance also spans a wide range, even surpassing that of the actual sports car on some models although on most it is quite modest, with the emphasis on sporty appearance.

Nissan's Sentra based NX 2000 is a particularly attractive sportcoupe

The Tercel-based Paseo is Toyota's entry in the sportcoupe market

Toyota's Celica is another attractive sportcoupe

Sportcoupe
(continued)

The Volkswagen Cabriolet is a sporty convertible model

The Ford EXP sportcoupe combines economy with sports car-like handling

The Nissan 240SX sportcoupe is a rear-wheel drive design

Many people with large families find the a full-size van to be good alternative to a station wagon

Full-size vans

Once relegated strictly to the delivery business, the full-size van utility vehicle is becoming increasingly popular as a primary vehicle for many because of the extra room it provides. As with other truck based designs, in recent years the manufacturers have made full-size vans more comfortable, quiet and car-like in handling so they will have wider appeal. The major drawback to these models; poor gas mileage, has been improved in recent years by computer-controlled engines.

This short wheelbase Dodge Ram 150 offers a good compromise between the mini- and full-size vans

When Chrysler developed the mini-van on a front drive passenger car chassis, they launched a whole new category of vehicle

An alternative to the common mini-van is this Volkswagen Vanagon camper with its stand-up headroom and obvious camping advantages

Mini-van

When Chrysler introduced the mini-van in 1984, a whole new category of vehicle was born. Several millions in sales later, the mini-van is now a staple of the auto industry and virtually every manufacturer has some version of this design. Usually based on front drive car (Ford Windstar) or rear drive mid-size truck chassis (Chevrolet Astro), the minivan fills a real need for young families and others who require the space the box-like interior provides. The car-like handling and interior versatility of the mini-van has helped hasten the demise of the conventional station wagon.

The versatility of interior space use has been one of the mini-vans secrets of success

The interior on most modern mini-vans is car-like and often very luxurious

Sport Utility Vehicles come in all sizes like this Suzuki Sidekick

Two-wheel drive SUV's, such as this Toyota 4Runner, are popular with people who don't need four-wheel drive

Sport-utility vehicles

The four-wheel drive (4WD) sport-utility vehicle (SUV) is an increasingly popular type of vehicle. To the surprise of many manufacturers, the SUV has struck a chord among the driving public, perhaps because it is perceived as rugged, reliable and safe. Most are never driven off road and in response to this fact most manufacturers offer two-wheel drive versions. The drawbacks to SUV's are that they have less usable interior space, use more gas because they weigh more, and are less stable than two-wheel drive sedans of comparable size and performance. Because of their popularity, you will pay a premium for a used SUV.

Many SUV's have racks on the roof for carrying extra luggage or equipment

The Jeep Wrangler is a sporty SUV

Another advantage of full-size SUV's is they can tow sizable loads

Mini-trucks are practical and economical

The bed on this Toyota T100 is designed to accommodate four-by-eight foot plywood sheets

Pick-up trucks

Pick-up trucks have consistently outsold all other vehicles. They're simpler, more rugged and, because of the pick-up bed, more useful than a car to people who need to haul plywood, sheet rock, dirt bikes, bicycles, camping equipment, etc. Later models are surprisingly car-like in comfort and amenities. Another important consideration is the fact that pick-up trucks are the only vehicles with sufficient capacity to tow heavy loads. Since they are based on older technology whose tooling has long since been amortized, pick-ups tend to be more inexpensive and can be among the best used vehicle bargains.

Large pick-up trucks such as this dual-wheel Dodge club cab are capable of hauling and towing heavy loads

The Dodge Dakota mid-size pick-up is available with a V8 engine

Passenger capacity

Think about *how many people you have to haul around most of the time*. Don't buy a sports car that seats two if you're planning to have two kids before it's paid for. Don't buy a full-sized crew-cab duallie pick-up if you just need something to get you to work. Generally, the bigger and more spacious the car, the worse the fuel mileage. And when you're shopping for cars in the classifieds, watch out! The Environmental Protection Agency (EPA) rates passenger capacity by the *number of seat belts installed*. But this isn't too realistic: Some cars with six pairs of seat belts won't really seat six adults, or even five adults, in any reasonable degree of comfort. If you're looking for a car that seats three adults in the back seat, put two other adults in the back seat, then hop in yourself. Then think about putting three people back there on a lengthy commute.

Even though it is a compact, this Volkswagen Jetta has a useful trunk

Cargo volume

Think about the size and shape of the cargo you're going to carry. An architect or an artist who carries large portfolios back and forth between home and office would have a hard time finding a place to put their portfolios in a Mazda Miata or a Toyota MR2. But they might fit fine in some other sports car, say one with a hatchback and a fold-down rear seat. Look at the depth and width of the cargo area carefully and realistically.

Engine size

If, for instance, you are a commuter and fuel economy is your primary criterion for picking the right power plant, a small, four-cylinder engine will deliver better mileage than a V6 (but it will also produce less performance). Sometimes, however, a small engine in a large vehicle will produce poor performance *and* poor fuel economy because the small engine has to work harder than a large engine.

If performance is of paramount importance, a larger engine will usually outperform a smaller engine (but it will also produce poorer fuel economy). But this picture is no longer as clear as it once was. Some modern high-performance fours with double-overhead cam, 16-valve heads and/or turbocharging, are approaching V6 performance. Meanwhile, some high-performance six-cylinder engines using similar technology are encroaching on the performance envelopes of the V8.

Front-wheel drive (FWD) or rear-wheel drive (RWD)?

Front-wheel drive (FWD) vehicles have a lighter, more compact drivetrain leaving more room inside for the passengers and cargo. FWD cars also provide better traction when driving on winter roads covered by ice and snow. However, FWD vehicles can be more difficult to service because everything - engine, transaxle (transmission and differential in one assembly) and driveshafts - is crammed under the hood. And some FWD parts are both more difficult to replace and more expensive to buy.

For example, most FWD cars use MacPherson struts instead of separate coil springs and shock absorbers at the front; some FWD cars use struts at the rear too. Struts are more expensive and more difficult to replace than shocks and springs. And the wheels must be aligned when the struts are replaced. What was once an inexpensive job on a conventional RWD car has now become a moderately expensive job on a FWD car.

Another example: Constant velocity (CV) joints in the driveaxles of FWD cars have taken the place of U-joints in the driveshafts of RWD cars. No one would argue that CV

The outer constant velocity (CV) joint boots on front-wheel drive cars deteriorate under normal driving and can eventually require expensive repairs

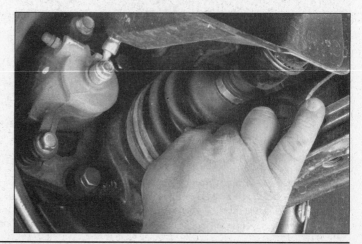

On a typical front-wheel drive vehicle, the engine is said to be mounted transversely (side-to-side) in the engine compartment. The front of the engine (the end on which the drivebelts are located) is facing to one side of the vehicle

On a typical rear-wheel drive vehicle, the engine is mounted longitudinally (end-to-end). The front of the engine (drivebelt end) is facing to the front directly behind the radiator. Be aware that a few front wheel drive vehicles with longitudinally mounted engines have been manufactured, if your unsure which you're looking at, look under the vehicle for a driveshaft connecting the transmission to the rear axle (rear-wheel drive vehicle)

joints are not superior to U-joints, but they cost about five times as much. There are two CV joints per driveaxle on a FWD car. The cost of replacing both CV joints could run quite high.

And RWD cars? They're usually bigger, heavier and use more fuel than FWD cars. Which is why there aren't too many of them left in the new car ranks. Nearly all new vehicles use FWD. RWD has become the exclusive refuge of the upscale luxury car and the expensive Asian or European luxury performance sedan. There are very few moderately priced RWD vehicles left on the market place. Nevertheless, there are still a wide variety of used full-size and mid-size RWD cars available. Some used car buyers may consider relatively poor mileage a worthwhile tradeoff for more power, luxury and comfort. And some buyers just don't feel safe in a smaller car.

The Nissan Quest is a version of the Mercury Villager and made in the U.S.

Domestic or import?

In recent years, some Japanese vehicles have earned consistently high marks from marketing analysts and from respected consumer groups. If resale value is important, some Japanese and European cars have held their value better than most American cars for quite some time. However, the build quality and craftsmanship of American cars has improved significantly during the last decade, and some models are closing the gap with the imports.

Repair costs are another factor to consider. European imports have fewer sales so have fewer dealers. If you plan to pay a professional to maintain your used European car, be aware that some of these models are more expensive to service. And even if you plan to do your own maintenance, bear in mind that import parts tend to be considerably more expensive, and harder to get, than for domestic and many Japanese models, particularly those for low-volume models such as Audi, BMW, Mercedes, Porsche, Saab and even Volvo.

At any rate, in the emerging global economy, the "world car" (a single platform for the three major markets, manufactured locally and tailored to local tastes and trends) renders the concept of a "domestic" or "import" model meaningless. For example, BMWs are made in South Carolina, Chrysler LH models are made in Canada, Volkswagens are made in Mexico, Hondas and Toyotas are made in the USA, etc. It's virtually impossible to label a modern vehicle as 100 percent American or Japanese or European. A car with a foreign nameplate might have just as many domestic parts in it as does a vehicle with a domestic nameplate.

Base or loaded? Economy or luxury?

For some people, there's no such thing as too much luxury, especially if it doesn't add too much to the purchase price of a good used vehicle. But before buying a used car that's loaded with luxury items, here are some things to consider: First, if the car is older and you intend to keep it for awhile, plan on fixing some of those gizmos at some point (or having them fixed). You can still drive the car with a broken cruise control or lock and unlock the doors with a defective power door lock mechanism. But if power window or power seat motors fail - which they do on older vehicles - there's no manual override, so they must be fixed immediately. And repairs can be expensive.

So, if economical operation is your primary criterion, and you plan to hang onto the car for a few years, a plain-Jane base model is the way to go. It will cost less to buy and be cheaper to operate. If you intend to resell the car before it's worn out, however, a luxury model may be the way to go, because it will be easier to sell.

Safety considerations

The old saw about full-size American luxury cars being safer than smaller import vehicles is notwithstanding, there are some other factors to take into account when considering the safety of the vehicle you're buying. It's certainly true that a large vehicle will sustain less damage than a smaller vehicle in a collision between the two. The vehicle with the

If the vehicle you're looking at has a larger than normal steering wheel center section with the letters SRS imprinted on it, it's equipped with an airbag

straint System), SIR (Supplemental Inflatable Restraint) or something similar. An airbag warning light on the instrument panel should glow when the ignition key is turned ON and should go out a few seconds after the engine is started. If it stays on or comes on while driving, a problem with the system is indicated. If the vehicle you're considering for purchase has an airbag, or airbags, have your professional mechanic check it out to make sure it's still operational. And, if you're a do-it-yourselfer, you should know that driver's side airbags make working around the steering wheel a little more dangerous, i.e. they *can* accidentally deploy. Be careful to follow the manufacturer's instructions for disabling the airbag module when working around the dash and steering wheel or near the airbag system sensors.

The anti-lock brake system (ABS) is also becoming a familiar sight on newer vehicles. The system is electronically controlled and prevents the vehicle from skidding in a panic stop situation. It is a proven fact that a vehicle can stop shorter if the brakes are applied in a controlled fashion and not allowed to lock-up. A vehicle equipped with ABS can usually be identified by the letters ABS imprinted on the brake pedal pad or by a molding or decal on one of the exterior body panels. An ABS warning light on the instrument panel should glow when the ignition key is turned ON and should go out a few seconds after the engine is started. If it stays on or comes on while driving, a problem with the system is indicated. There are already a host of late-model used vehicles on the market with first-generation ABS. From the standpoint of safety, ABS is a wonderfully effective option. However, from the standpoint of do-it-yourself maintenance, it's well beyond the scope of the average home mechanic. If you buy a used vehicle with ABS, and it malfunctions, count on taking the vehicle to a dealer to have it repaired. ABS systems are both complex and expensive to repair.

Airbags and ABS are here now. In the future, all cars will have these features. So, despite their complexity and expense, both are valuable options if you're considering a late-model used vehicle, particularly if you intend to resell the car within a few years.

greater mass absorbs less of the impact energy. Larger vehicles also have more sheet metal to absorb some of the impact. And statistics from the Insurance Institute for Highway Safety indicate that fatality rates are directly proportional to vehicle size. See the *Helpful Resources* section at the end of this book for the address of the Insurance Institute of Highway Safety and other consumer safety groups, if you would like results of these crash tests. The rate for smaller vehicles (under a 95-inch wheelbase) is more than double that for full-size vehicles. Of course, if you collide with an immovable object such as an overpass or an Armco barrier at speeds above 35 mph, your chances of escaping unscathed are slim, regardless of the size of the vehicle in which you're traveling.

There are several other factors which you should consider, too, besides size and weight. Another factor worth considering is the design of the vehicle itself. Some buyers place a high priority on purchasing a vehicle that gives them better odds in a serious accident. For example, in crash tests, some smaller vehicles, such as the Saab 900, have fared better than larger vehicles. Another factor to consider is that you might be able to avoid an accident in the first place in a smaller, nimbler car that can stop and handle better than a larger vehicle.

Once you're *in* an accident, however, airbags and seat belts are just as important as the size or construction of a vehicle. When shopping for a used car, inspect the seat belts carefully. There should be one seat belt per occupant and they should be in good shape. Seat belts are still the first line of defense in an accident for most vehicles.

Federally mandated, airbags are installed on more and more late-model used vehicles. A car with a driver's airbag will have a larger than normal center section of the steering wheel. Also somewhere on the steering wheel or dash panel you will find imprinted the letters SRS (Supplemental Re-

First-year models

There was an old adage about not buying a vehicle that's manufactured on Monday or Friday, because more of the plant workers are absent on those days and those who were there were less attentive. Modern production techniques have changed this. A more modern adage is that you should avoid buying a vehicle built in the first year after a major redesign, especially if the engine and drivetrain are all new. Is this adage true? Well, in recent history there are a few examples of where "all-new" vehicles had some initial bugs that had to be worked out, but most have no more problems than subsequent years of the same design. Consumer publications such as *Consumer Reports* can help you identify vehicles that have problems by design.

Where to buy a used car

New car dealers

Believe it or not, franchised new-car dealers are one of the safest places to buy a late-model used car. Dealers usually acquire a good number of the vehicles on their used car lot as trade-ins; often, some of these vehicles were initially sold right out of their new-car showroom and were maintained in their own service department. Why would dealers be concerned about the condition of the vehicles on their used car lot? Because they have a reputation to protect, and they know that there are legal remedies you can pursue if they defraud you. Besides, they want to stay on your good side so you'll buy parts and service from them. And because they have a service department, dealers often include a modest warranty (30-day/1000 miles, or similar terms) when they sell a used car.

Other advantages? The used cars at new-car dealer lots usually have good titles (if they don't, you have legal recourse). And if you're looking for longer-term financing, the dealer can probably provide it (although the interest rate and terms may not be as good as a bank).

Of course, there are a few disadvantages to buying from a new-car dealer. The sales staff is savvy and well-trained, so it will be more difficult to negotiate a great deal. Also, the selection will be limited if you're looking for a particular older model; the used cars at new-car dealerships tend to be later-model vehicles. And a new-car dealer often asks more for the same used vehicle than a private party or used car lot.

Used car dealers

You can usually cut a better deal at a used car lot, which is normally a lower-overhead operation with no on-site repair facilities. There will be a wider variety of older models to look at than you would find at a new-car dealer, but the selection is sometimes older and less appealing than at a new car lot. There are a few other advantages when buying from a used car dealer: Some credit is usually available (though it is usually short-term). The dealer is licensed, so he's accountable, just as a new-car dealer is. And the used cars should have a good title.

The chief disadvantage of buying from a used car dealer is that there tend to be more used car dealers that engage in fraud and misrepresentation than new car dealers. This is not to say that there aren't many good used car dealers that can give you an honest deal, but be more cautious.

If you're thinking about buying from a used car lot, here's an alternative: Have a look at vehicles offered by neighborhood service stations that sell used cars as a sideline. Like new-car dealers, they tend to sell vehicles they've serviced, and, like dealers, they have a reputation to pre-

serve. In any case, if you decide to shop at used car lots, choose one that has been at the same location for a while; shady operators tend to move around a lot.

Car rental agencies

Rental agencies tend to sell their vehicles a year or two after they buy them and can be a source of good late-model used cars. This is especially true if you're in the market for plain-vanilla daily drivers such as small sedans and compacts. These used cars will likely have been driven hard with minimal maintenance, but will probably still have a fairly low mileage reading on the odometer. Some rental agencies routinely replace high-wear parts like brakes and tires before offering the cars for sale. Some provide buyers with complete, detailed maintenance records from their fleet service department.

Look up rental companies in the yellow pages of your phone book and give them a call.

Banks

Banks and other lenders also enter the used car business occasionally with repossessed vehicles - or "repos" as they're called in the used car business. Sometimes, they've been abused; you can't count on a repo to be in the best condition. If its former owner couldn't make the payments, it's unlikely taking good care of the car was a high priority either. However, since their main line of business is not cars, lenders usually like to get rid of cars quickly, so you can often get a good deal.

Private party

Because private sellers have essentially no overhead, they aren't concerned with markups, and are usually inexperienced at sales so their prices are generally lower than those of a new or used car dealer. This type of transaction is potentially the friendliest, most comfortable and convenient way to buy a used vehicle. Also you stand a better chance of getting an actual record of repair and maintenance from a conscientious private seller.

However, a private seller isn't going to give you a written guarantee, and you can't expect any help from a private seller if the car breaks down shortly after buying it. You may be on slightly surer ground if you buy the car from a relative, friend or neighbor, because you at least know it's history. But such transactions have been known to strain valued relationships. And don't forget that you'll have to handle the registration paperwork yourself with a private-party purchase.

If you decide to buy a used car from a private seller, you may have to drive all over town looking at a small number of examples of the type of vehicle you're hoping to find. And when you get there, some models may bear only a passing resemblance to their published description in a newspaper classified ad or auto trader. Both prices and quality can be wildly inconsistent when dealing with private sellers. Besides, even if you find a car you like, keep in mind that a private party is not a licensed dealer (or at least he's not supposed to be), so he is not required to provide any sort of guarantee. If the vehicle turns out to be a bad buy for some reason or immediately breaks down, you have no recourse. Needless to say, there's no financing available.

It's also remotely possible to get bad paper (unclear title to the vehicle) when buying from a private party. When buying from a private party, make sure he has the title paper and that it is authentic (study the title paper from another car to be sure). Also make sure the Vehicle Identification Number (VIN) on the title matches the VIN on the car. To be absolutely sure the owner is the real owner, ask to see his driver's license. There have been cases where an individual will buy a problem car for the sole purpose of re-selling, then never register it. When he sells it to you, he gives you the paperwork signed by the previous owner. In this scenario, the seller protects himself from any actions by you.

Dealer-only auctions

Another way to buy a used car is to buy it at a dealers-only auction through a licensed dealer. Before discussing the pros and cons of a dealer-only auction, it's important to understand that a dealers-only auction is not the same thing as a public auction. Let's look at the difference between the two. Auctions open to the public are usually advertised on the back page of the classified section of the newspaper. These auctions are outlets for used city police vehicles, local government vehicles, etc. They're sometimes disguised as "drug seizure" auctions because it pulls in the customers who think they're going to walk out with an outrageous deal on a Porsche or Ferrari (actually very, very few of the vehicles sold at these auctions are drug seizures).

A dealers-only auction is open only to licensed dealers who are registered to do business with that auction house. The public is not allowed to attend. The vehicles come from everywhere: Bank "repos" (repossessions), leased cars, factory demos, theft recoveries, dealer "overflow" (slow sellers), banks, etc. The dealers at these auctions are looking for rock bottom prices on cars they want to buy for resale on their lots. Because dealers stop bidding long before the bidding frenzy on a vehicle pushes its asking price anywhere near retail (they don't even like to pay Blue Book wholesale, but prefer to pay hundreds less), there is little danger that the vehicle will go for any more than that. And the selection is huge. Typically, dealers-only auctions range from 500 to almost 3000 cars. You can find anything you want at one of these auctions, which are held weekly.

When you buy through a licensed dealer at a dealers-only auction, you are buying through a licensed dealer. If something goes wrong, you have legal recourse. Even if a dealer moves, the state department of motor vehicles (or whatever it's called in your state) can find him because he is

Five questions to ask before you look at the vehicle

Particularly when dealing with private parties (who usually have only one car for you to look at), you'll want to make sure a vehicle is worth your time before you make the drive. Always call first and talk to the owner/driver - other people in the house may not be able to answer all your questions.

1 **Why are you selling the vehicle?** You're probably not interested, but a person selling the vehicle because of mechanical problems will often stumble on this question, alerting you to look at the vehicle very carefully.

2 **How many miles are on the odometer?** Generally speaking, multiply the year age of the vehicle by 15,000. If the vehicle has more miles on it than the product of this equation, the vehicle is usually considered to have high mileage.

3 **What condition is the vehicle in?** Actually, this should be a series of questions like "how's the body and paint?," how's the interior?", etc. You'll find that a seller's opinion will often differ greatly from yours once you see the vehicle, but you can often discover problems like accident damage. This may save you a trip if you're looking for an unmolested vehicle.

4 **What work has been done on the vehicle recently?** Sellers often "prepare" a vehicle for sale by performing work they've been meaning to do for a while. This is usually an innocent attempt to make the vehicle look more appealing, but be a bit wary if major work has just been completed. For example, if the engine has just been overhauled, make sure the engine is checked out thoroughly. It's rare, but owners occasionally try to get rid of a vehicle that's showing signs of slipshod workmanship on a major repair.

5 **What options does it have?** This will actually be a series of questions pertaining to your needs (it's a good idea to make a list before you start making calls). For example, if you need an automatic transmission or air conditioning, make sure you ask whether the vehicle has these options. Ask which engine the vehicle has. A friend may have told you of the great fuel economy of his car, but the same model with a different engine option may not do so well. Always be sure you're making an apples-to-apples comparison.

bonded, and the threat of legal action against his license is sufficient to force him to back down if he breaks the law.

Titles are guaranteed at dealers-only auctions. If you buy a car through a dealers-only auction, you know you're getting a car that's not stolen and can be traced. There's also less chance of fraud than in a private-party sale. Dealers-only auctions have some built-in protections such as disclosure of mileage, mileage deficiencies, frame damage, fees owing, etc. And most auctions have some sort of drivetrain guarantee on certain makes and models.

Naturally, there are some disadvantages to a dealers-only auction, just as there are disadvantages to any type of sale. To buy a car at auction, you must pay cash. Which means you either have enough cash or you arrange financing ahead of time. Another disadvantage is that you will have little opportunity to inspect and no opportunity to test drive the vehicle before buying it. That's one reason why cars go for so little money at a dealers-only auction - they're being purchased "as is." And if your dealer gets the highest bid on the car you want, it's yours. Federal and state consumer laws designed to protect consumers who change their mind after purchase don't apply to auction vehicles. Once you buy it, you can't change your mind. If you want to get rid of it, you'll have to sell it.

Some people who make their living buying and selling cars for private clients consider dealers-only auctions the best combination of getting a good deal at a great price. So how do you get in on it? First, you must locate a good dealer to inspect the car thoroughly and to represent you well at the auction. This must be a dealer you can trust, who is honest and who charges a fair commission. A tall order, but do-able. Word-of-mouth recommendations are the best endorsement. Try to avoid walking into a dealership seeking a dealer you can trust!

Once you've lined up the dealer you wish to hire as your representative at the auction, here's how it works: He will arrange to meet you at the auction most likely to fill your needs, and together the two of you will inspect dozens, perhaps hundreds, of vehicles and pick out the most interesting example(s). At this point, you and the dealer will probably want to settle on his fee and discuss how much you want to spend for the vehicle you want. He'll may help you clarify what it is you really want and discuss possible bargains for certain types of vehicles currently going for below market value. Then you'll give him a good faith down payment, say 20 percent of the vehicle's estimated going price. Using your funds, he buys the car you want at the next auction if he can do so within the agreed upon price range. If necessary, he'll have the car smogged, cleaned up and/or repaired as necessary. Then the paperwork is completed and the car is transferred to you. His fee and any costs (taxes, licensing, smog, repairs, etc.) are deducted from the 20 percent down payment. Any other fees owed to the dealer are paid to him at this time; any funds left over are returned to you. And that's it! Simple.

Recalls

Recalls are repairs suggested by automobile manufacturers and the National Highway Traffic Safety Administration (NHTSA) to ensure the safety or mechanical integrity of your automobile. These repairs are necessitated by some factory defect or oversight, and, as such, they are done free of charge by any new-car dealership authorized to sell the type of car you own. Since a used car owner is usually unaware of a recall, you can find out whether a recall exists for your car by calling NHTSA at 1-800-424-9393, or you can write directly to the manufacturer at the address provided in your owner's manual. If there happens to be a recall involving your particular vehicle, have it serviced as soon as possible. Some recalls are for serious conditions like failing brakes or spontaneous engine fires, and there's no sense gambling with your safety.

Technical service bulletins

Every year the divisions that make up the three major domestic automotive corporations (Chrysler, Ford and General Motors) as well as the various foreign auto makers send hundreds of documents called Technical Service Bulletins (TSB's) to the service departments of new-car dealerships. TSB's provide the dealership mechanics with information about specific, common problems with particular car or truck models, engine types, transmission types, etc.

TSB's keep dealership mechanics up-to-date on the latest troubleshooting and repair information and they alert the mechanics to recently designed parts, give pertinent details concerning new repair or maintenance procedures, or sometimes even revise information given in the vehicle's shop manual. TSB's are important because they are the primary means by which the automotive manufacturers communicate the solutions to potential problems you may experience with your car or truck.

Technical Service Bulletins do not apply exclusively to new cars. They often apply to cars that are several years old, and there is no time limit after which they expire or are no longer issued.

A word of caution concerning TSB's: Because mechanics at dealerships are normally paid in accordance with the number of cars they service per day, they sometimes don't make full use of TSB's. Some are reluctant to search their TSB files for pertinent information on your car because, to them, time is money and such research is frequently time-consuming. If you request them, he must show them to you (of course, he is under no obligation to pay for copies or even to make copies; unless you're on very good terms with your dealer, you should offer to make, and to pay for, a duplicate set of copies). It is important for you to insist on TSB's while your car is still under warranty because any necessary mechanical corrections will of course be done for free.

Warranties of various types are available on used cars

Warranties

A warranty repair is any work done on a vehicle at a dealership facility under the terms listed in the owner's manual. Many times, there's no charge for the work done, but there may be a modest deductible once the specified mileage or time limit has been exceeded. Warranties have changed dramatically since their inception, from the standard "12 months or 12,000 miles" (12/12) to the long-term, comprehensive protection currently offered by manufacturers. As new-vehicle prices continue to climb, customer demands have pushed manufacturers to provide better and better product coverage.

Warranty coverage can be confusing on vehicles that are leased, sold or traded. The general rule here is that warranty coverage *stays with the vehicle, not with the owner*. For awhile, some manufacturers insisted on a "transfer fee," but most of them have since changed their policies in an effort to improve customer satisfaction. When buying a used vehicle, you should know that any remaining factory warranty coverage (but *not* aftermarket "service contracts" or extended warranties) still applies to the vehicle *regardless of a change in ownership*. But be aware that while warranty coverage may still exist, *transfer* of the warranty must be completed before it goes into effect.

Unlike a new car, a used vehicle is no longer protected by a manufacturer's warranty, if it has reached the time limit or the mileage limit specified under the terms of the original warranty. However, some new-car buyers purchase an extended warranty, which may still be in effect at the time the car is sold to a second owner. Such warranties may be transferable, but there's often a fee. Always ask the original owner about the terms of coverage, spelled out in both the manufacturer's standard and extended warranties.

All new vehicles now come with a federally-mandated, extended emissions warranty which covers virtually every fuel, ignition and emission component. This warranty is generally longer than the manufacturer's warranty.

The Used Car Rule and the FTC Buyers Guide label

In 1985, the federal government passed a law known as the Used Car Rule. The Rule, which is enforced by the Federal Trade Commission (FTC), requires that every used car sold by a dealer must have a "Buyers Guide" label with pertinent warranty information on one of its windows. The FTC produces this window sticker, which states whether a warranty is included with the car, what type of warranty it is, and other information required under the Used Car Rule. It also warns that all promises should be in writing. The Buyers Guide actually serves as part of the official sales contract. Inspect the Buyers Guide label closely. There are three boxes: "AS IS - NO WARRANTY," "WARRANTY," and "IMPLIED WARRANTIES ONLY."

As Is

The term "AS IS" constitutes a denial of warranty coverage, except in Connecticut, Massachusetts, Minnesota, New York, and Rhode Island where dealers *must* warranty all but the oldest, cheapest cars. You will pay all costs for any repairs. The dealer assumes no responsibility for any repairs regardless of any oral statements about the vehicle.

Warranty

The term "WARRANTY" means that the dealer will pay some percent of the labor and some percent of the parts for the covered systems that fail during the warranty period. Ask the dealer for a copy of the warranty document for a full explanation of warranty coverage, exclusions, and the dealer's repair obligations. Under the law, "Implied warranties" may give you even more rights.

Implied Warranties Only

The term "IMPLIED WARRANTIES ONLY" means that the dealer does not make any specific promises to fix anything (even things that need to be repaired) when you buy the vehicle or after the time of the sale. But, state law "Implied warranties" may give you some rights to have the dealer take care of serious problems that were not apparent when you bought the vehicle.

Manufacturer's standard warranties

At one time, the standard manufacturer's warranty was 12 months or 12,000 miles, whichever came first. If anything broke during the first year of operation, it was fixed free of charge. There was no deductible. After the initial time or mileage was exceeded, the warranty covered the "powertrain" (engine, transmission/transaxle, driveline, differential, rear axle, and transfer case, if equipped) up to 24 months or 24,000 miles. There was usually a $100 deductible. This setup was the industry standard for decades. Eventually, this $100 deductible powertrain coverage was bumped up to 36 months or 36,000 miles. Later, as manufacturers began to view the warranty as a marketing device, they added the term *bumper to bumper*, usually for the length of 36/36,000. A bumper-to-bumper warranty included all the items covered in the initial 12/12,000 warranty, but it included a $100 deductible.

The terms of standard warranties on today's cars are longer than ever, both in miles and months. When you shop for a used vehicle, look closely at the actual written terms of the standard warranty. If it's still in effect, it should cover everything, including the powertrain, cosmetic things such as interior and exterior trim, and all electrical devices and systems. It should also include a corrosion warranty, which covers all damage caused by rust. A competitive powertrain warranty should be at least 5 years or 50,000 miles, and some manufacturers are even going to 7/70,000. Look for warranty coverage (sometimes as much as 100,000 miles) protecting the finish and/or the body from corrosion, rust and *environmental fallout* (rail dust, smog, factory emissions, acid rain, etc.).

When you're buying a used vehicle, ask the seller to show you the actual written terms of any warranty that came with the vehicle when it was new. Ask him whether you have any options, such as a choice between a higher-mileage warranty with a deductible versus an all-inclusive bumper-to-bumper warranty with no deductible, but shorter terms.

Extended warranties and service contracts

Extended warranties are sold through dealerships. They can be backed by either the manufacturer or by an aftermarket company. The cost of purchasing an extended warranty can be high. Make sure you get your money's worth. The coverage spelled out in an extended warranty often "overlaps" the terms of the standard manufacturer's warranty. During the initial period already covered by the manufacturer, the only additional benefit available may be the use of a rental vehicle during repairs.

An extended warranty does not have to be purchased at the time you purchase a new vehicle. In most cases, you have 12 months or 12,000 miles (the terms of the original standard manufacturer's warranty) to buy an extended warranty. Ask the salesman for information regarding various extended warranty plans. Have him spell out in writing what you'll be getting if you buy an extended warranty, and ask him to show you the difference between the manufacturer's standard warranty and the extended warranty.

The Federally-mandated extended emissions warranty

Because of its wide-ranging coverage, the Federally-mandated extended emissions warranty can offer powerful protection to the buyer of a late-model used car. First, because of the sheer length of its coverage it's probably the *only* warranty that's likely to still be in effect by the time a car is sold to a second owner. Second, it covers virtually all of the fuel, engine electrical and emissions systems, so some of the most expensive parts on the car are protected.

So before you dive under the hood to troubleshoot or fix a problem related to emissions, there are some things you should know about the Federally-mandated extended warranty, which is designed to protect you from the cost of repairs to *any* emission-related failures beyond your control.

There are actually TWO emission control warranties - the "Design and Defect Warranty" and the "Performance Warranty." We will discuss them separately.

The Design and Defect Warranty

Basically, the Design and Defect Warranty covers the repair of all emission control related parts which fail during the term of the warranty. According to Federal law, the manufacturer must repair or replace the defective part free of charge if:

a) It is within the term of the warranty;
b) An original equipment part or system fails because of a defect in materials or workmanship; and
c) The failure would cause your vehicle to exceed Federal emissions standards.

If these three conditions are present, the manufacturer must honor the warranty. All manufacturers have established procedures to provide owners with this coverage. The Design and Defect Warranty applies to used vehicles too. It doesn't matter whether you bought the vehicle new or used; if the vehicle hasn't exceeded the warranty time or mileage limitations, the warranty applies.

The Design and Defect Warranty applies to all vehicles, including cars, pick-ups, recreational vehicles, heavy-duty trucks and motorcycles. The length of the warranty varies somewhat with the type of vehicle. If you own some type of vehicle other than a car, read the description of the emissions warranty in your owner's manual or warranty booklet to determine the length of the warranty on your vehicle.

What parts or repairs are covered by the warranty?

Coverage includes all parts whose primary purpose is to control emissions and all parts that have an effect on emissions. Let's divide these two types of parts in two categories - emissions-control parts and emissions-related parts - then divide the parts within each category into systems. Our list would look something like this:

Primary emissions control parts

Air induction system
Thermostatically controller air cleaner
Air box

Air injection system
Diverter, bypass or gulp valve
Reed valve
Air pump
Anti-backfire or deceleration valve

Early Fuel Evaporative (EFE) system
EFE valve
Heat riser valve
Thermal vacuum switch

Evaporative emission control system
Purge valve
Purge solenoid
Fuel filler cap
Vapor storage canister and filter

Exhaust gas conversion systems
Oxygen sensor
Catalytic converter
Thermal reactor
Dual-walled exhaust pipe

Exhaust Gas Recirculation (EGR) system
EGR valve
EGR solenoid
EGR backpressure transducer
Thermal vacuum switch
EGR spacer plate
Sensor and switches used to control EGR flow

Fuel metering systems
Electronic control module or computer
    command module
Deceleration controls
Fuel injectors
Fuel injection rail
Fuel pressure regulator
Fuel pressure dampener
Throttle body
Mixture control solenoid or diaphragm
Air flow meter
Air flow module or mixture control unit
Electronic choke
Altitude compensator sensor
Mixture settings on sealed carburetors
Other feedback control sensors, switches and valves

Ignition systems
Electronic spark advance
High energy electronic ignition
Timing advance/retard systems

Miscellaneous parts
Hoses, gaskets, brackets, clamps and other accessories used in these systems.

Positive Crankcase Ventilation (PCV) system
PCV valve
PCV filter

Emissions-related parts

The following parts have a primary purpose other than emissions control, but they still have a significant effect on your vehicle's emissions. If they break or malfunction, your vehicle's emissions may exceed Federal standards, so they're also covered by the Design and Defect Warranty. They include:

Air induction system
Turbocharger
Intake manifold

Carburetor systems
Carburetor
Choke

Exhaust system
Exhaust manifold

Fuel injection system
Fuel distributor

Ignition system
Distributor
Ignition wires and coil
Spark plugs

Miscellaneous parts
Hoses, gaskets, brackets, clamps and other accessories used in the above systems

If, after reading the list above and the manufacturer's description of your warranty coverage in your owner's manual or warranty booklet, you're confused about whether certain parts are covered, contact your dealer service department or the manufacturer's zone or regional representative.

Can any part of a warranty repair be charged to you?

No! You can't be charged for any labor, parts or miscellaneous items necessary to complete the job when a manufacturer repairs or replaces any part under the emissions warranty. For example, if a manufacturer agrees to replace a catalytic converter under the emissions warranty, you shouldn't be charged for the catalyst itself or for any pipes, brackets, adjustments or labor needed to complete the replacement.

How long does the warranty apply?

Parts which don't have a replacement interval stated in the maintenance instructions are warranted for what the EPA calls the "useful life" of the vehicle, which, for cars, is, as stated before, five years or 50,000 miles. For other types of vehicles, read your warranty description in the owner's manual or the warranty booklet to determine the length of the warranty coverage.

Other parts, for example those with a stated replacement interval such as "15,000 miles or 12 months," are warranted only up to the first replacement.

Any parts that are the subject of a maintenance instruction that requires them to be "checked and replaced if necessary," or the subject of any similar requirement, are warranted for the entire period of warranty coverage.

How do you know if you're entitled to coverage?

If you or a reliable mechanic can show that a part in one of the listed systems is defective, it's probably covered under the emissions warranty. When you believe you've identified a defective part that might be covered, you should make a warranty claim to the person identified by the manufacturer in your owner's manual or warranty booklet.

What should you do if your first attempt to obtain warranty coverage is denied?

a) Ask for the complete reason - in writing - for the denial of emissions warranty coverage;

b) Ask for the name(s) of the person(s) who determined the denial of coverage;

c) Ask for the name(s) of the person(s) you should contact to appeal the denial of coverage under the emissions warranty.

Once you've obtained this information, look in your owner's manual or warranty booklet for the name of the person designated by the manufacturer for warranty assistance and contact this person.

How does maintenance affect your warranty?

Performance of scheduled maintenance is YOUR responsibility. You're expected to either perform scheduled maintenance yourself, or have a qualified repair facility perform it for you. If a part failure can be directly attributed to poor maintenance of your vehicle or vehicle abuse (proper operation of the vehicle is usually spelled out in your owner's manual or maintenance booklet), the manufacturer might not be liable for replacing that part or repairing any damage caused by its failure. To assure maximum benefit from your emissions control systems in reducing air pollution, as well as assuring continued warranty coverage, you should have all scheduled maintenance performed, or do it yourself.

Do you have to show any maintenance receipts before you can make a warranty claim?

No! Proof of maintenance isn't required to obtain coverage under the emissions warranty. If a listed part is defective in materials or workmanship, the manufacturer must provide warranty coverage. Of course, not all parts fail because of defects in materials or workmanship.

Though you're not automatically required to show maintenance receipts when you make a warranty claim, keep receipts just in case.

How is your warranty affected if you use leaded gasoline in your vehicle?

When leaded gas is used in vehicles designed to run on unleaded, the emissions controls - particularly the catalytic converter - can be damaged. And lead deposits inside the engine can lead to the failure of certain engine parts. The emissions warranty does not cover ANY part failures that result from the use of leaded fuel in a vehicle that requires unleaded fuel.

Can anyone besides dealers perform scheduled maintenance recommended by the manufacturer?

Absolutely! Scheduled maintenance can be performed by anyone who is qualified to do so, including you (as long as the maintenance is performed in accordance with the manufacturer's instructions). If you're going to take the vehicle to a repair facility, refer to your owner's manual or maintenance booklet and make a list of all scheduled maintenance items before you go. When you get there, don't simply ask for a "tune-up" or a "15,000 mile servicing." Instead, specify exactly what you want done. Then make sure the work specified is entered on the work order or receipt that you receive. This way, you'll have a clear record that all scheduled maintenance has been done.

If you buy a used vehicle, how do you know whether it's been maintained properly?

Realistically, you don't. But it never hurts to ask the seller to give you the receipts which prove the vehicle has been properly maintained according to the schedule. These receipts are proof that the work was done properly and on time, if the question of maintenance ever arises.

And once you buy a used vehicle, you should continue to maintain it in accordance with the maintenance schedule in the owner's manual or warranty booklet (If the seller doesn't have these items anymore, buy new ones at the dealer).

What should you do if the manufacturer won't honor what you feel is a valid warranty claim?

As we said earlier, if an authorized warranty representative denies your claim, you should contact the person designated by the manufacturer for further warranty assistance. Additionally, you're free to pursue any independent legal actions you deem necessary to obtain coverage. Finally, the EPA is authorized to investigate the failure of manufacturers to comply with the terms of this warranty. If you've followed the manufacturer's procedure for making a claim and you're still not satisfied with the manufacturer's determination, contact the EPA by writing:

Warranty Complaint
Field Operations and Support Division (EN-397F)
U.S. Environmental Protection Agency
Washington, D.C. 20460

The Performance Warranty

The Performance Warranty covers those repairs required because the vehicle has failed an emission test. If you reside in an area with an Inspection/Maintenance program that meets Federal guidelines, you may be eligible for this additional Performance Warranty. For more information on the Performance Warranty, ask your local Inspection/Maintenance program official or call or write the nearest EPA office and ask for a copy of the pamphlet "If Your Car Just Failed An Emission Test . . . You May Be Entitled To Free Repairs," which describes the Performance Warranty in detail.

You may be eligible for coverage under this warranty if:

a) Your car or light truck fails an approved emissions test; and

b) Your state or local government requires that you repair the vehicle; and

c) The test failure didn't result from misuse of the vehicle or a failure to follow the manufacturer's written maintenance instructions; and

d) You present the vehicle to a warranty-authorized manufacturer representative, along with evidence of the emission test failure, during the relevant warranty period; then

e) For the first two years or 24,000 miles, whichever comes first, the manufacturer must pay for all repairs necessary to pass the emissions test; and

f) For the first five years or 50,000 miles, the manufacturer must pay for all repairs to primary emission control parts which are necessary to pass the emissions test.

What vehicles are covered by the Performance Warranty?

The Federally mandated Performance Warranty covers all cars and light duty trucks produced in the last five years. And it doesn't matter whether you bought your vehicle new or used, from a dealer or from a private party. As long as it hasn't exceeded the warranty time or mileage limitations, and has been properly maintained, the Performance Warranty applies.

What types of repairs are covered by the Performance Warranty?

Two types of repairs are covered by the Performance Warranty, depending on the age of your vehicle:

1 Any repair or adjustment which is necessary to make your vehicle pass an approved locally-required emission test is covered if your vehicle is less than two years old and has less than 24,000 miles.

2 Any repair or adjustment of a "primary emissions control" part (see "The Design and Defect Warranty") which is necessary to make your vehicle pass an approved locally-required test is covered if your vehicle is less than five years old and has less than 50,000 miles. Although coverage is limited after two years/24,000 miles to primary emission control parts, repairs must still be complete and effective. If the complete and effective repair or a primary part requires that non-primary parts be repaired or adjusted, these repairs are also covered.

What if the dealer claims your vehicle can pass the emissions test without repair?

The law doesn't require you to fail the emissions test to trigger the warranty. If any test shows that you have an emissions problem, get it fixed while your vehicle is still within the warranty period. Otherwise, you could end up failing a future test because of the same problem - and paying for the repairs yourself. If you doubt your original test results or the dealer's results, get another opinion to support your claim.

What kinds of reasons can the manufacturer use to deny a claim?

As long as your vehicle is within the age or mileage limits explained above, the manufacturer can deny coverage under the Performance Warranty only if you've failed to properly maintain and use your vehicle. Proper use and maintenance of the vehicle are your responsibilities. The manufacturer can deny your claim if there's evidence that your vehicle failed an emissions test as a result of:

a) Vehicle abuse, such as off-road driving, or overloading; or

b) Tampering with emission control parts, including removal or intentional damage; or

c) Improper maintenance, including failure to follow maintenance schedules and instructions, or use of replacement parts which aren't equivalent to the originally installed part; or

d) Misfueling: The use of leaded fuel in a vehicle requiring "unleaded fuel only" or use of other improper fuels.

If any of the above have taken place, and seem likely to have caused the particular problem which you seek to have repaired, then the manufacturer can deny coverage.

If your claim is denied for a valid reason, you may have to pay the costs of the diagnosis. Therefore, you should always ask for an estimate of the cost of the diagnosis before work starts.

Can anyone besides a dealer perform scheduled maintenance?

Yes! Scheduled maintenance can be done by anyone with the knowledge and ability to perform the repair. For your protection, we recommend that you refer to your owner's manual to specify the necessary items to your mechanic. And get an itemized receipt or work order for your records.

You can also maintain the vehicle yourself, as long as the maintenance is done in accordance with the manufacturer's instructions included with the vehicle. Make sure you keep receipts for parts and a maintenance log to verify your work.

Why maintenance is important to emissions control systems

Emission control has led to many changes in engine design. As a result, most vehicles don't require tune-ups and other maintenance as often. But some of the maintenance that is required enables your vehicle's emission controls to do their job properly. Failure to do this emissions-related maintenance can cause problems. For example, failure to change your spark plugs during a 30,000-mile tune-up can lead to misfiring and eventual damage to your catalytic converter.

Vehicles that are well-maintained and tamper-free don't just pollute less - they get better gas mileage. Which saves you money. Regular maintenance also gives you better performance and catches engine problems early, before they get serious - and costly.

How do you make a warranty claim?

Bring your vehicle to a dealer or any facility authorized by the manufacturer to perform warranty repairs to the vehicle or its emissions control system. Notify them that you wish to obtain a repair under the Performance Warranty. You should have with you a copy of your emissions test report as proof of your vehicle's failure to pass the emissions test. And bring your vehicle's warranty statement for reference. The warranty statement should be in your owner's manual or in a separate booklet provided by the manufacturer with the vehicle.

How do you know if your claim has been accepted as valid?

After presenting your vehicle for a Performance Warranty claim, give the manufacturer 30 days to either repair the vehicle or notify you that the claim has been denied. If your inspection/maintenance program dictates a shorter deadline, the manufacturer must meet that shorter deadline. Because of the significance of these deadlines, you should get written verification when you present your vehicle for a Performance Warranty claim.

The manufacturer can accept your claim and repair the vehicle, or deny the claim outright, or deny it after examining the vehicle. In either case, the reason for denial must be provided in writing with the notification.

What happens if the manufacturer misses the deadline for a written claim denial?

You can agree to extend the deadline, or it may be automatically extended if the delay is beyond the control of the manufacturer. Otherwise, a missed deadline means the manufacturer forfeits the right to deny the claim. You are then entitled to have the repair performed at the facility of your choice, at the manufacturer's expense.

If your claim is accepted, do you have to pay for either the diagnosis or the repair?

You can't be charged for any costs for diagnosis of a valid warranty claim. Additionally, when a manufacturer repairs, replaces or adjusts any part under the Performance Warranty, you may not be charged for any parts, labor or miscellaneous items necessary to complete the repair. But if your vehicle needs other repairs that aren't covered by your emissions warranty, you can have that work performed by any facility you choose.

What happens to your warranty if you use leaded gasoline?

When leaded gas is used in vehicles requiring unleaded, some emission controls (especially the catalyst) are quickly damaged. Lead deposits also form inside the engine, decreasing spark plug life and increasing maintenance costs.

If your use of leaded fuel leads to an emissions failure, your warranty won't cover the repair costs. So using leaded fuel will not only ruin some of your emission controls, it will cost you money.

Can your regular repair facility perform warranty repairs?

If you want to have the manufacturer pay for a repair under the Performance Warranty, you MUST bring the vehicle to a facility authorized by the vehicle manufacturer to repair either the vehicle or its emission control systems. If your regular facility isn't authorized by the manufacturer, tell your mechanic to get your "go-ahead" before performing any repair that might be covered by the Performance Warranty.

Do you have to provide proof of maintenance when you make a warranty claim?

You're not automatically required to show maintenance receipts when you make a warranty claim. But if the manufacturer feels your failure to perform scheduled maintenance has caused your emissions failure, you can be required to present your receipts or log as proof that the work was in fact done.

If you buy a used vehicle, how do you know whether it's been properly maintained?

When you buy a used vehicle, try to get the maintenance receipts or log book from the previous owner. Also ask for the owner's manual, warranty or maintenance booklet, and any other information that came with the vehicle when it was new. If the seller doesn't have these documents, you can buy them from the manufacturer.

To guarantee future warranty protection for your vehicle, conform to the maintenance schedule provided by the manufacturer.

Does the warranty cover parts that must be replaced as a part of regularly scheduled maintenance?

Parts with a scheduled replacement interval that's less than the length of the warranty, such as "replace at 15,000 miles or 12 months," are warranted only up to the first replacement point. Parts with a maintenance instruction that requires them to be "checked and replaced if necessary," or some similar classification, receive full coverage under the warranty. However, should you fail to check a part at the specified interval, and should that part cause another part to fail, the second part will NOT be covered, because your failure to maintain the first part caused the failure.

The manufacturer may or may not require that such replacement parts be a specific brand. But if a test failure is caused by the use of a part of inferior quality to the original equipment part, the manufacturer may deny your warranty claim.

What if the manufacturer won't honor a claim you believe to be valid?

First, use the information contained above to make your case to the dealer. Then follow the appeals procedure outlined in your vehicle's warranty statement or owner's manual. Every manufacturer employs warranty representatives who handle such appeals. The manufacturer must either allow your claim or give you a written denial, including the specific reasons for denying your claim, within 30 days, or you are entitled to free repairs.

Also, the Environmental Protection Agency is authorized to investigate the failure of manufacturers to comply with the terms of this warranty. If you've followed the manufacturer's procedures and you're still unimpressed with the reason for denial of your claim, contact the EPA at:

Warranty Complaint
Field Operations and Support Division (EN-397-F)
U.S. Environmental Protection Agency
Washington, D.C. 20460

Finally, you're also entitled to pursue any independent legal actions which you consider appropriate to obtain coverage under the Performance Warranty.

Financing

Paying cash is the best way to buy a used car, but this is not always practical. If you are going to finance the car, it's wise to arrange this financing before you go car shopping. Dealer financing is often not the best way to go, so check rates and terms at banks, credit unions, etc. before you go shopping so you'll have something to compare the dealer financing to.

If the dealer interest rate is appreciably lower than what you can obtain elsewhere and you intend to keep the car for the full term of the loan, it may be worth negotiating with the dealer for financing.

Trade-in value

If you have a car to trade in, this is actually the first step of price negotiation. Settle the value of the trade-in first, as a separate issue, without mentioning the price of the car you are going to buy. Once what you feel you have arrived at a fair amount, write it down and have the salesperson acknowledge and (if possible) initial it. This amount is set aside as to reduce sale price. Be sure you've checked newspaper ads and, if you can get ahold of one, a Kelly Blue Book, to verify what a fair price is.

Sale price

Determining the sale price is always the problem with buying a used car, whether negotiating with a private party or a dealer. On dealer lots an innocuous tag or sticker can usually be found on the vehicle with a coded price. The salesperson has only to glance at the this tag to instantly know what the price is. The vehicle price is usually buried in an otherwise meaningless string of numbers but if you can break the code, you will be able to begin the negotiation on even terms with the salesperson.

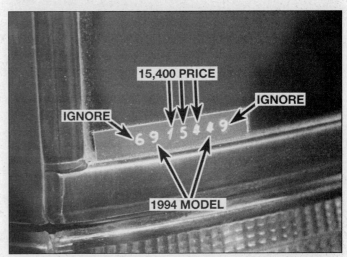

If you can decipher it, this small tag can tell you that this vehicle is a 1994 model and the asking price is $15,400

Monthly payment

Remember, the monthly payment must be something that you can live with. Don't sign anything until you are sure what the monthly payment is, how much each payment is and when the first and last payments are due. You must also know how much the prepayment penalty is and how it is determined.

Down payment

Once you have determined the price and the monthly payment amount you want, the down payment in cash is used to reduce the amount owed and thus the monthly payments.

Loan amount

You need to know exactly what the total due or borrowed amount of the loan is and how much the closing or any other costs are.

Payment period

Make sure that you know what the length of the loan is in months, what the grace period is, when a payment becomes late and what the late payment charge is.

Annual percentage rate (APR)

You must know what the annual percentage rate (APR) is for the loan. Sometimes a dealer or bank will quote a lower, add-on rate instead. A 6% add-on rate, for instance, is actually around 11% APR.

Total car cost

Add up the sale price, finance charges, tax and license fees to arrive at the total car cost.

Vehicle Identification Number (VIN)

Refer to the Vehicle Information Number (VIN) guide at the end of this manual for important information on your car or truck. The VIN number is a long string of numbers and

The Vehicle Identification Number (VIN) is located on a plate visible through the driver's side windshield

letters imprinted on a small plate on the driver's side of the dashboard. These are the numbers by which the state in which the vehicle is licensed and registered. But what most people *don't know* is that those numbers mean a lot more than simply the "identification number" of a vehicle. Once you know what each individual number represents, you can learn all sorts of information about a vehicle.

Referring to the information at the back of this manual, you can determine which engine a vehicle is equipped with (or was originally equipped with) and verify the vehicle is the advertised model year.

2 The Walk-around Inspection

The minimum used car buyer's "hunting outfit" might consist of these items:

1. Blanket
2. Checklist
3. Notebook and pen
4. Rubber hose for listening
5. Screwdrivers
6. Known-good cassette tape
7. Tape measure
8. Flashlight
9. Paper towels

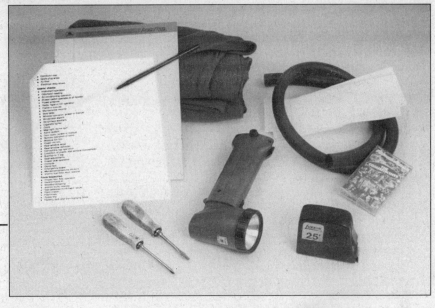

Why a walk-around?

The purpose of the walk-around inspection is to get a quick and accurate idea of the overall condition of the car. By the time you've completed this preliminary inspection, you'll be able to decide whether it's worth spending some more time looking at the car more closely or whether you should eliminate it from further consideration because of some fatal flaw such as:

a) Excessive collision damage
b) Rust or structural damage to the body or frame
c) An engine or drivetrain that's worn out
d) An interior that's in poor condition
e) Any defect that's unacceptably expensive to fix

During the walk-around inspection, you'll be looking for these and other flaws that mean "walk away and look for another car." But there are also a couple of other categories of problems that might or might not ax the deal, depending on the seller's attitude.

If you discover problems that look somewhat less than terminal, but still must be fixed, jot them down, go away and try to estimate as accurately as possible what it's going to cost to fix them before going any further. Consult with your mechanic if necessary. The cost of fixing less-than-terminal-but-nevertheless-serious problems must be deducted from the seller's asking price. If he doesn't agree to do so, walk away.

If you find evidence of the type of nagging little problems that are relatively minor in the larger scheme of things, but are nevertheless annoying, look at them as legitimate reasons to deduct the cost of repairing them from the seller's asking price (even if you have no intention of actually ever fixing them!).

Used car inspection tools

When inspecting a used car take along the following tools and supplies:

1) **Notebook and pen or pencil** - take notes on everything that looks wrong, sounds funny or smells bad

A friend with automotive knowledge is an invaluable aid when choosing a car, new or old

Your friend may notice something like this - a truck without a rear bumper - this may be legal in some states and not in others, and buying a new bumper will be necessary if you plan to tow anything

2) **Checklist** - photocopy the checklist at the end of this Chapter

3) **Flashlight** (or drop light that runs off the car battery) - the engine compartment and the underside of the car will be dark and dirty

4) **Screwdriver** - a small screwdriver will be useful for performing many of your checks

5) **Several shop rags or paper towels** - for wiping off your hands and cleaning components you'll want to inspect

6) **Old blanket or towel** - you'll need to lie down on the ground to check the underside of the vehicle for oil leaks, worn or damaged components, etc.

7) **Short section of clean rubber hose or plastic tubing** - a 12 to 16 inch piece of tubing makes a good "stethoscope" for listening to the engine or other components for unusual noises

8) **Tape measure or small steel ruler** - handy for measuring things like the distance from each wheel to the wheel well

9) **Cassette tape and/or Compact Disc** - for testing the cassette player and/or CD player

If the vehicle passes the walk-around, you may want to include the following tools for the more detailed inspection described in Chapter 4:

1) **Small toolbox with a ratchet and socket set, a spark plug socket, miscellaneous screwdrivers, a pair of pliers and a tire tool** - if you're more mechanically inclined and time and space allows, you may want to check the brakes, spark plugs, etc.

2) **Small magnet** - used for checking body panels for plastic body filler

3) **Multimeter** - for making minor electrical tests

Bring a friend

The only other "tool" you should try to bring is a mechanically-inclined friend, preferably one who's more mechanical than you are. It's always good to get a second opinion. Two heads are definitely better than one when trying to identify a used car's flaws. Besides, your friend won't be as emotionally involved with the car as you are. And if the car gets past this walk-around inspection, you can have your friend tag along in a second car in order to watch what comes out the tailpipe and other tasks which we'll discuss in the next Chapter.

Likewise, if you are shopping for a car in a state in which there are annual or semi-annual inspections, make sure the car has passed the tests and has a current sticker on the windshield

Is the seller willing to allow a mechanic to inspect the car?

Before proceeding with the walk-around inspection, ask the seller whether he's willing to let you have a professional mechanic check out the car before you make a final decision to buy it. In most cases the seller will agree, if time is available and the situation allows it. If the seller refuses without an apparent reason, be very careful before proceeding further, he may be hiding a serious problem which he's afraid a mechanic will find.

Look at the engine

Pop the hood and look at the engine. Is it clean? Or is it covered in oil and dirt? Is it rusty? Does it have damaged or missing parts? Does it have loose wires, cables, vacuum lines or anything else that looks like it should be attached, connected or plugged in somewhere? A dirty or rusty en-

Besides looking at the condition of the tires (no kicking!), consider the suitability - if you are looking at sport-utility vehicles but don't plan any off-roading, you'll want mild-mannered treads, not noisy all-terrain tires

Typical engine compartment components locations

1 Engine oil dipstick	6 Windshield washer fluid reservoir	12 Serpentine drivebelt routing decal
2 Automatic transmission fluid dipstick	7 Air cleaner housing	13 Radiator hose
3 Engine oil filler cap	8 Power steering fluid reservoir	14 Battery
4 Crankcase ventilation system hose	9 Radiator cap	15 Relay box
5 Brake fluid reservoir	10 Drivebelt	16 Coolant reservoir
	11 Distributor cap and wires	17 Vehicle Emissions Control Information label

If an engine is dirty, rusty or coated with grease and grime, chances are it's not going to be in as good condition as it should

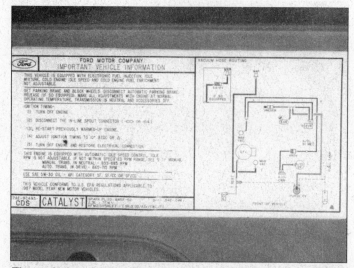

The underhood emission information decal should be in place under the hood or on the fan shroud - you or your mechanic may need it later for engine diagnosis or tuning

gine, a missing or damaged part, a bunch of disconnected vacuum hoses - these aren't necessarily grounds for dismissal. But when you find this kind of neglect without really trying, what it's telling you is: Be wary of this car. The owner didn't take very good care of it. And an engine that looks bad will often run badly as well. You want to pay very close attention to a dirty, oily, rusty engine or one that's missing parts.

Tip

If the emissions information decal is missing, you can usually order a new one from the dealer parts department.

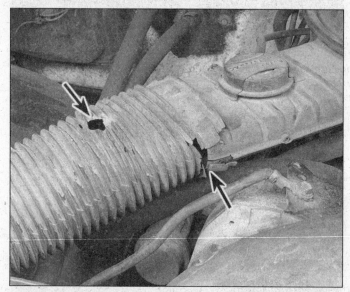

Make a note of every damaged part you find on the engine; they'll provide you with bargaining power when negotiations begin. For example, this intake duct is worn out and should be replaced, and the current owner should bear that cost, not you. Of course, the owner probably won't want to actually go out and buy the part, but should discount the asking price for the car by that much to cover it

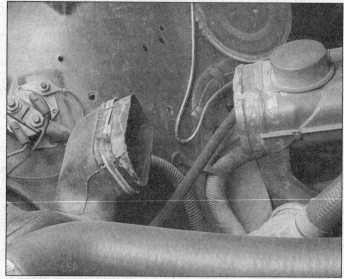

The intake duct between the fresh air inlet and the air cleaner housing is missing from this engine. This is the kind of missing part you need to remember when it comes time to negotiate, in some states this car would not pass a vehicle or smog inspection

This battery is so new it's still covered in plastic, but the owner forgot to install a hold-down device of any type, so the battery is adrift on its tray.

Believe it or not, the cooling system on this car still worked despite the condition of the radiator. This radiator has clearly outlived its usefulness.

You'll find the oil filler cap somewhere on the valve cover. If the engine is a longitudinally-installed V6 or V8, the cap could be on either valve cover; if the engine is a transverse installation, the oil filler cap will always be on the front valve cover. Some oil filler caps on older vehicles have a hose running to the PCV filter in the air cleaner housing (left photo); later caps have no hose but are clearly marked (right photo). Always make sure the area around the opening is clean before unscrewing the cap to prevent dirt from contaminating the engine

Check the oil

Find the oil filler cap. It's almost always located on top of the valve cover on inline four and six-cylinder engines, or on one of the valve covers on V6 and V8 engines. Unscrew the oil filler cap, turn it upside down and look at it. The oil may look brand new. Don't be surprised. Sellers often change the oil before putting a used car on the market. Or the oil on the bottom of the cap may look used and even dirty, but that's okay. What's not okay is the underside of a cap coated by a light brown frothy sludge with the appearance and consistency of a chocolate milkshake! There may also be small droplets of water or coolant mixed with the oily sludge. This condition indicates coolant has gotten into the oil from a failed gasket, or worse yet, a cracked cylinder head or block. Whatever the case, the vehicle should not be driven far, or at all, until the condition is repaired. Oil conta-

If the underside of the oil filler cap looks like a chocolate milkshake, coolant has escaped past a blown head gasket and mixed with the oil. An engine with a condition such as this will require immediate repair and possibly a complete overhaul

Check the oil level on the dipstick - it should be at or near the upper hatched area on the dipstick; if it isn't, have the owner top it up before you start the engine or test drive it (it takes one quart of oil to raise the level from the lower to the upper mark). If the oil level is low, make a note of it and have your mechanic look this engine over very carefully to determine whether it's been damaged by an oil level that's been too low for too long

Inspect the coolant in the reservoir; make sure it's clean and near the full mark. If the coolant is low, have the owner top it up before you test drive the car. If it has pieces of debris floating in it, or a darker sludge at the bottom of the reservoir, have your mechanic check out the entire engine cooling system

taminated by coolant can do a lot of damage in a short time to the internal engine components. A repair of this sort is usually quite expensive and, if severe enough or neglected, could require a complete engine overhaul. If you spot something unusual and feel you are not experienced enough to make a definite diagnosis of the condition, proceed carefully and insist on having the vehicle inspected by a professional mechanic.

If the oil on the underside of the cap looks okay, pull out the dipstick and look at the oil level. It should be full. If it isn't, look under the vehicle for spots of oil on the ground; the engine may be leaking. Make a note of it and have your mechanic look the engine over very carefully (see Chapter 5). He'll test the engine's compression and do a cylinder leak-down test to make sure none of the piston rings, valves or head gasket is damaged by a low oil level. In the meantime, don't even start the engine until the owner or seller adds the specified oil.

Check the coolant

As long as you're looking at the engine's vital fluids, take a quick peek at the coolant in the reservoir. It should

be a greenish color (some coolant is red, however) and have kind of a sweetish smell. If the coolant looks more like water than like coolant, there may be a leak somewhere and the owner has simply added water over and over to refill it (of course, this means the coolant's boiling point is lowered and the cooling system boils over spewing even more coolant). Make sure the coolant doesn't smell like gasoline or oil; if it does, the engine may have a blown head gasket. If the coolant is low, ask the owner or seller to add coolant before you start the engine.

> **Tip**
>
> If the vehicle is close to your home, try showing up at an unexpected time so the owner won't have a chance to warm the engine and otherwise prepare the vehicle.

> **Tip**
>
> If you see oil floating on top of the coolant, either the engine is seriously damaged, has a blown head gasket or the transmission oil cooler is ruptured. Both are major repairs, so take this into consideration before deciding on the vehicle.

Is the engine cold?

Feel the upper radiator hose or the valve cover. They should be cold; if they're already warm when you arrive to inspect the car, the owner may have warmed up the engine to hide cold-starting or warm-up problems, or other difficulties. Go ahead and perform the walk-around inspection but make a note to come back and inspect the engine cold before making a final decision.

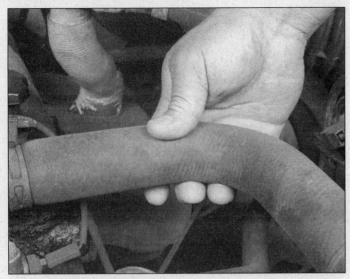

How do you know whether the engine was warmed up before you arrived? Feel the upper radiator hose; if it's hot or warm, the engine has been run in the last hour

Was the engine run over an hour before you arrived? One way to tell is to feel the valve cover (the engine cylinder head retains heat longer than the radiator hoses)

Where there's smoke . . .

Start the engine. Does it start easily? An elaborate starting ritual indicates problems. If the engine is hard to start, make a note to have your mechanic take a closer look to determine whether it's a starting system problem, or a fuel or ignition problem.

As you start the engine, look out the rear view mirror and note whether smoke pours out the tailpipe. If it does, proceed with caution. Please note: We're not talking about a puff or wisp of smoke that appears - then just as quickly disappears - when a car is started; that's normal. What we're talking about is a big, billowing cloud of smoke. There are three kinds of smoke to watch for:

a) **Black smoke** - Black smoke means that the fuel system is delivering too much fuel. In other words, the air-fuel mixture is too rich and the engine is unable to burn it all. Black smoke doesn't necessarily disqualify the vehicle from consideration. If the car runs rich, but turns out to be a gem in most other ways, jot it down and brief your mechanic. He may find that a simple adjustment will rectify the situation. But have him inspect the catalytic converter closely. When an engine runs rich, the raw fuel in the exhaust gas causes the catalytic converter to become a catalytic furnace. It makes no difference whether the rich condition is caused by a couple of misfiring spark plugs or a couple of leaking injectors; in either case, raw fuel is pumped directly into the converter. This raises the operating temperature of the converter to dangerous levels. Over a period of time, higher operating temperatures can cause a converter to break up or melt down.

b) **Blue smoke** - Blue smoke means the engine is burning oil. This is a definite disqualifier! Reconsider a vehicle that's burning oil unless you're buying it as a project vehicle and intend to rebuild the engine anyway.

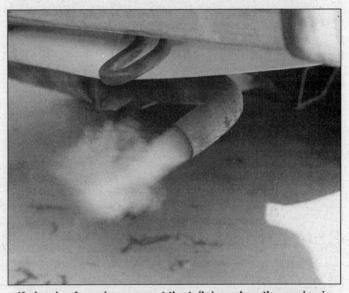

If clouds of smoke pour out the tailpipe when the engine is started, the color of the smoke can tell you a lot about the condition of the engine: Either the engine is running rich (black smoke), burning oil (blue smoke) or allowing coolant to leak into one or more of the combustion chambers (white smoke); black smoke may mean nothing more than a tune-up is needed, but blue or white smoke are usually reason enough to just say no to this car

c) **White smoke** - White smoke means the engine is burning the coolant (antifreeze and water) from its own cooling system. It probably has a blown head gasket which is allowing coolant to seep from a cooling passage into a combustion chamber. The only other explanation for white smoke is very cool and humid ambient air (low dew point). This phenomenon is similar to the condensation of your breath in very cold weather; when your breath is much warmer than the ambient air, it condenses as it mingles with the colder ambient air, producing steamy vapors. In a similar fashion, hot exhaust gases mingle with the cool and humid ambient air to produce white smoke (steam), but it should dissipate as the car warms up because hot exhaust gases have a lower moisture content. Of course, if you're looking at a used vehicle in a very, very cold climate (say, Bemidji, Minnesota in the winter!), the engine exhaust may continue to condense even after it's warmed up! Use your judgment here. If you're looking at white smoke on a warm day, it could indicate some sort of mechanical problem. If you're looking at white smoke on a freezing day, it might not mean anything; if you're unsure, jot it down and remind your mechanic to check it out. If you're seeing white smoke on a day that's somewhere in between the two extremes, wait and see what happens once the engine is fully warmed up. Then make your decision accordingly or jot down a note to remind yourself to brief your mechanic of the situation.

Large amounts of white smoke emitted while the car is being driven can be an indication of a transmission problem, not coolant. Many automatic transmissions have a vacuum line running up to the engine. If a seal or diaphragm is leaking at the transmission end of this vacuum line, automatic-transmission fluid can be sucked into the engine, making copious exhaust smoke. The fix for the leak is easily taken care of, but the transmission may have suffered serious damage if the leak has gone on for any length of time.

If the engine emits big clouds of black, blue or white smoke, proceed with caution. If it's really cold outside and you're not sure whether the white smoke issuing forth from the tailpipe is normal or not, jot it down for your mechanic to check later.

The engine should now be idling smoothly. Tap the throttle. The engine should respond without hesitation and return to idle without bogging or stalling. Turn off the engine and restart it. It should restart as easily as it did the first time. Put the shift lever in Park (automatics) or Neutral (manual transmission), apply the parking brake and leave the engine running. There are some other things you need to check while the engine is warming up.

What's that funny noise?

Get out of the car and open the hood. Listen carefully for any unusual noises such as chafing, chirping, clicking, knocking, rubbing, rumbling, screeching or squealing sounds. Rev up the engine, then quickly release the accelerator several times. Note whether these noises rise and fall with engine speed. Clicking noises that rise and fall with engine rpm can be expensive repairs like valve or piston damage, or they can be nothing at all, like clicking fuel injectors. Lower end (crankshaft/connecting rod) problems are usually characterized by a deep knocking or rumbling sound. The bearings in most externally-mounted components (wa-

> **Tip**
>
> It's sometimes difficult to tell whether noises in an engine compartment are coming from the engine itself or one of the accessories attached to the engine, such as the alternator or power steering pump. Hold a piece of rubber hose to your ear and move the other end of the hose among the components attached to the engine – this will often help isolate the source of the noise. Be very careful not to contact moving or hot components or you may hurt yourself.

ter pumps, air conditioning compressors, power steering pumps, etc.) usually make a screeching, squealing or chirping sound when they're worn out. Even though you may not have the trained ear of a professional mechanic, you "know" what your own car sounds like. And you know that an absence of strange sounds is good.

If you hear really loud, conspicuous sounds, and the engine runs poorly on top of that, be very careful before proceeding any further. If you hear noises that sound kind of funny, but the engine seems to be running well otherwise, or if you hear noises that seem to subside as the engine warms up, jot them down in your notebook for further investigation by your mechanic. Try to describe what they sound like, where they're coming from, and whether they rise and fall with engine speed. (And keep in mind that the results of this walk-around inspection, the test drive and the detailed mechanical inspection may be overshadowed by what your mechanic tells you.)

What's that funny smell?

While the engine is idling, note whether you can smell exhaust inside the car. If so, several bad things have probably happened. First, the exhaust manifold, the exhaust pipes or the muffler is leaking. That's not necessarily a fatal - or an expensive - flaw, but what produces the odor *is* expensive. Some part of the car's floor has rusted through, or has been damaged by an accident, and is allowing leaking exhaust gases to enter the passenger compartment. Unless the car has an awful lot going for it, you may want to rule it out.

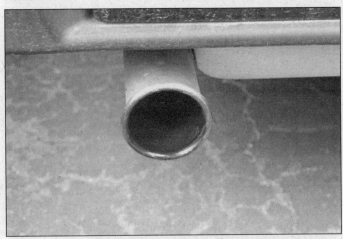

Black, gummy deposits on the inside of the tailpipe indicate the engine is burning oil

If you find white or tan deposits on the inside of the tailpipe, the fuel system is delivering an air-fuel mixture that's too lean

What does the tailpipe tell you?

Here are two other easy tests you can do: Go to the rear of the car and inspect the tailpipe. Black, gummy deposits on the tailpipe indicate that the engine is burning oil; dry deposits indicate fuel-system problems. Now, put your hand over the tailpipe. A periodic burp or an uneven "spitting" sound may indicate valve or ignition problems. Here's an even better test: Take out a piece of your notebook paper and place it immediately behind the exhaust system tailpipe. If the paper is continually blown away by the exhaust gases, the engine is running normally. But if the paper is occasionally sucked towards the tailpipe, the engine may have major valve problems. A good running engine always blows exhaust gases *out* the exhaust system. An engine that alternately expels exhaust gases, then sucks air, has valve problems.

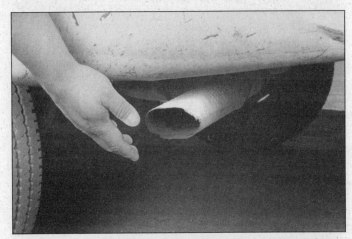

Put your hand over the tailpipe; if you can feel the engine "spitting" (making little "burps" or pulses), it's got an intermittent miss that could be caused by the valves, a jumped timing belt, an ignition or a fuel system problem

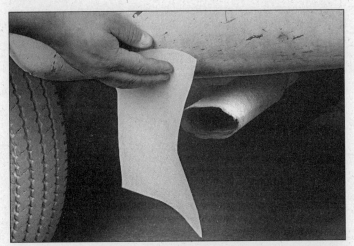

Put a piece of paper over the tailpipe and watch what it does: If the paper is continually blown away by the exhaust gases, the engine is okay, but if the paper is occasionally sucked towards the tailpipe, the engine may have major valve problems

You won't see much out the tailpipe tip on this truck, the pipe is rotted through - something that must be repaired as part of the purchase deal

After the engine has been running for five minutes, look underneath for any large pools of liquid; this small puddle is brake fluid that leaked from a master cylinder in a matter of minutes

Look for leaks

Turn off the engine. Get down on your hands and knees and look under the car for fresh pools of liquid.

a) Coolant is usually a greenish color (some manufacturers also use other dye colors) and it has a sweetish odor.

b) Engine oil is dark brown or black and has a burned odor.

c) Transmission and power steering fluid is a reddish color and has a sweetish odor.

d) Brake fluid is clear and also has a sweet odor.

One thing you'll notice right away, if you look at a lot of used cars, is that, except virtually-new, late-model used cars, *all engines seem to leak a little oil*. So don't start eliminating every car you find with a film of dirty oil covering the

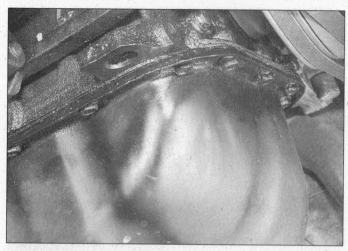

In the upper photo, the engine oil pan has a thin film of oil on it, but that doesn't automatically qualify it as a terminal leaker; it may simply be slowly weeping oil from the valve cover gasket and/or the oil pan gasket, both of which eventually allow oil to seep its way through. In the lower photo, the pan and even the subframe are covered in a thick, gooey layer of oil and road dirt. An engine with this much oil on it has a serious oil leak somewhere that should be fixed

> **Tip**
>
> Leaks are often difficult to locate, or see at all, when the vehicle is parked on blacktop or where leaks have previously soiled the paved surface. While the engine is running, place large pieces of clean cardboard under the engine and transmission or transaxle or drive the car and park it in a clean spot – even the smallest leak will be easily seen.

oil pan. Some oil is bound to leak out past the valve cover and/or the oil pan gaskets over tens of thousands of miles of driving. That type of leak can usually be fixed by replacing the valve cover and/or oil pan gasket and tightening the bolts to the correct torque specification.

What you're looking for are *large* leaks that pour steadily onto the ground. The kind that might be coming from a blown head gasket or a leaky front or rear main seal. Head gaskets and crankshaft seals are usually difficult to replace, even if the job can be done with the engine installed. Unless you're looking for a project, you don't want to inherit someone else's leaker. Walk away unless the seller is willing to have the leak fixed or reduce the price accordingly.

A late-model used car should have NO significant leaks. But older, higher-mileage engines do develop small leaks which ooze out between gasket mating surfaces (usu-

Most engines at dealerships will look brand-new, thanks to a steam-cleaning and detailing

To tell if it has been detailed, or actually well-kept by the original owner, push back hoses and lines to look at hidden areas where dirt may reside even after a quick detail job

ally between the valve cover and cylinder head, or between the block and the oil pan), migrate down the sides of the block and onto the pan, then slowly drip onto the ground. This type of leak is probably just a sign of old age. However, if you're wary of the way a leak looks, wipe off the surface of the engine in the vicinity of the leak, especially right below it, and then have another look at this area after the test drive. If you're still wary, jot it down and point it out to your mechanic. He'll help you decide whether, on balance, the car is worth buying despite the leak, or not.

Does the engine look too clean for a used car with its mileage? It's possible that the owner was the meticulous type who degreased the engine regularly. If so, you may be in luck. A do-it-yourselfer may have degreased his engine in order to do his own routine tune-ups and keep tabs on leaks large or small. The more likely possibility, however, is that the seller has just had the engine "steam cleaned." New and used car dealers typically steam clean the engine in a used car before putting it up for sale. Private sellers -

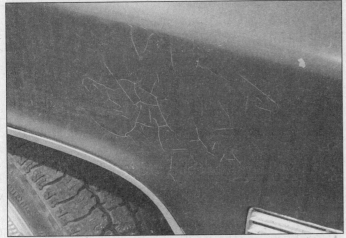

The cracks in the paint on this fender indicate poor bodyfiller work underneath, or a too-thick paint that is failing

aside from the aforementioned meticulous types - are less likely to do so.

One advantage of a steam-cleaned engine - besides the fact that it looks neat - is that a big leak is easier to spot when it flows, drips or runs across a clean engine surface. But steam cleaning also *erases* the evidence of any slow leaks. Once removed, a leak that occurred over a long period of time is unlikely to reoccur during the next hour or so. Fortunately, most dealers don't do all that good a job when they steam clean an engine; the top of the engine compartment looks shiny and spotless, but the underside may still be covered with grease and grime. So when you're looking for leaks, concentrate your inspection on the lower portion of the engine, because that's where the cumulative record of long-term leaks will appear.

Has the car been hit?

Look at the paint

If you're looking at older vehicles, some of them may have new paint jobs. In the southwest, cars are subjected to intense heat and sunlight which causes paint to fade. In smoggy areas, they're also bombarded by high levels of ozone, a corrosive compound produced by a combination of sunlight, volatile organic compounds (mainly hydrocarbons) and oxides of nitrogen. Ozone is a powerful agent: It breaks down paint coatings, dries out and rots rubber window molding and causes black plastic trim to fade to white. Some areas are exposed to acid rain, which also ruins paint. If a used vehicle is in reasonably good mechanical condition but its paint has been damaged by sunlight, ozone or acid rain, the owner may elect to apply a new paint job to make the car more attractive to potential buy-

Note how the painted surface on the left body panel has faded while the surface on the right still has a bright lustrous finish; when you see this kind of mismatch, look for the underlying reason why that panel was repainted

Pop the hood and look for signs of overspray around the edges of the engine compartment, or simply note whether the color of the engine compartment matches the color the car; this car was originally yellow (engine side), then was painted white (fender side)

ers. Fair enough. But beware of a late-model used vehicle with a new paint job. It may be suffering from serious rust or collision damage.

Look at the car in direct sunlight. Make sure the paint is all the same color. If the car has been repainted recently, mismatched colors will be fairly easy to distinguish in strong outdoor light. If half the car is slightly different in color from the other half, chances are the painted half has been hit, or has a serious rust problem. Why else would the owner have repainted only half the car? Most owners don't spend money to fix up a vehicle they intend to sell, unless they *have* to spend the money in order to get rid of it. Look carefully at body seam areas, since this is where partial-paint jobs from accident damage generally end.

There are several other ways to tell whether a car has been repainted:

a) Open the doors and note whether the edges of the doors and the door jambs match the new exterior paint color. If it's a really cheap paint job, they won't match, because having the door edges and jambs painted is an additional charge that some owners will be unwilling to pay for on a vehicle they intend to sell.

b) Look for paint overspray in the engine compartment or on the firewall; note whether the new paint color matches the color of the engine compartment and the underside of the hood. The engine compartment and hood are usually the same color as the original paint because the seller doesn't want to pay extra to have them prepped and painted. The cost of a paint job increases dramatically if the engine compartment is painted because everything must be removed prior to painting, then reinstalled afterwards.

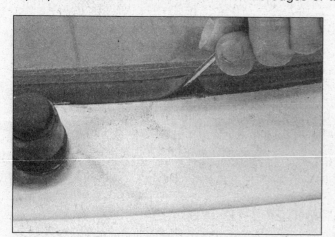

Lift the windshield molding to check for old paint underneath; very few owners are thorough enough to have the surfaces under the window molding repainted because that would mean removing all the molding first

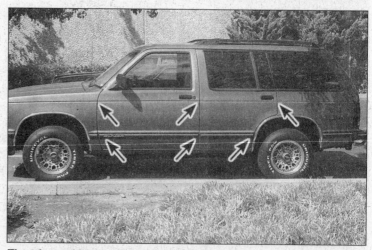

The trim and beauty lines (arrows) on a vehicle are an easy way to check for panel misalignment - each of these points should match from panel to panel

It may have been a simple bumper hit on this small car, but note how the quarter-panel is buckled - simply bending the bumper back isn't going to straighten the car

c) Let's suppose the seller did his homework. The door edges, doors jambs and engine compartment all match up. There's one more way to figure out whether the car was repainted. Lift up the edge of the windshield molding. The paint underneath will be the original paint, unless the owner has had all the molding removed prior to painting.

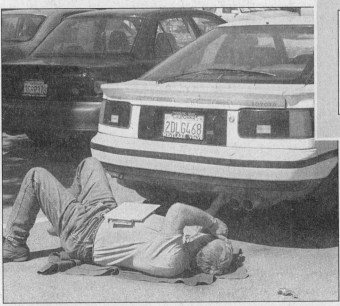

Look at the frame; is it obviously bent? It's virtually impossible to align the wheels on a car that has been hit hard enough to bend the frame. Are there welds across any of the frame members? If a car has been hit hard enough to break the frame, you would be better off looking elsewhere; the welds might be strong enough to prevent the frame from coming apart, or they might not

Finding body filler and thick paint

When minor rust or body damage has been repaired well, it is often difficult to tell there was ever a problem. Since body panels are not normally replaced for minor damage and rust, the usual checks for body panel alignment and overspray will probably not turn up anything.

As a careful buyer, you want to get the most unmolested vehicle possible. Plastic body filler that's used to repair dents and fill rusted-out areas eventually weakens and cracks. Also, even the best re-painting jobs are usually not as durable as the original factory job. When paint is too thick, it cracks and peels.

Pro Motorcar Products, Inc. has a unique tool called the "Spot Rot" gauge that is designed to find hidden body filler and paint that is thicker than 0.006-inch. The tool has a magnetic tip, calibrated spring and graduated body that allow you to quickly find these hidden body problems.

As an inexpensive (although not nearly as accurate) substitute for this tool, try a flexible refrigerator magnet. It's soft enough not to harm the paint, yet magnetic enough to do the job. Anywhere the magnet does not stick has body filler lying below the surface. Check extra carefully around the wheel wells, where rust damage is most prevalent.

Be aware that this procedure will not work on plastic body panels, bumper covers and several models that are presently manufactured from composite materials.

If you find no evidence of mismatched paint, a new paint job is always a big plus on an older used car. If you do find evidence of new paint, look for signs of poor body work or metal finishing. Sight along the body and look for irregularities in the sheet metal such as wavy or misaligned fender or quarter panels. If you find evidence of body work or poorly matched panels, doors, hoods, trunk lids, etc., the vehicle may have been hit so hard that these panels can be aligned. In other words, the frame may have been bent.

Look at the frame

Looking at the frame is a quick way to tell if the car has been hit hard. Lay your old blanket or tarp on the ground and sight along the frame rails or, on a car with a unit body, the reinforcing ribs. Is the frame obviously bent? Are there

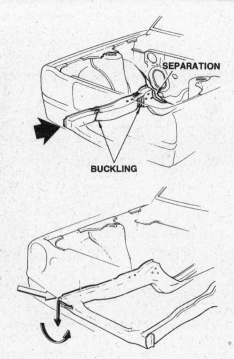

Unit body structures typically buckle at the front as shown here, check by measuring diagonally across the subframe

welds across any of the frame members? If so, the car has been hit hard.

Of course, the "frame" on most modern cars is no longer separate from the body. Modern cars are designed using "unit body" construction methods. A unit body is a body/frame design in which the body of the car, its floor pan and the chassis form a single structure. Such a design is generally lighter and more rigid than a car with a separate body and frame. Most trucks, vans and sport utility vehicles still have a separate frame and body, but some of the newest designs are also unit bodies. Nevertheless, even though there's no separate frame on a unit body vehicle, there are longitudinal reinforcing "ribs" running along the pan that serve the same function as frame rails. If a vehicle has been hit hard from either side or from either end at an angle, these reinforcing ribs will be bent.

How can you tell whether the car has been hit hard if the frame rails (or reinforcing ribs) show no obvious sign of damage? Perform the following simple test: Walk about 15 or 20 feet away from the front of the car, squat down and sight down both sides of the car, along the outside surfaces of the tires and wheels. The front and rear wheels should line up on both sides. Now go to the rear of the vehicle and do the same thing. The front and rear wheels should still line up. If they don't, the frame or the unit body is bent.

Even if the front and rear wheels on the left side and the

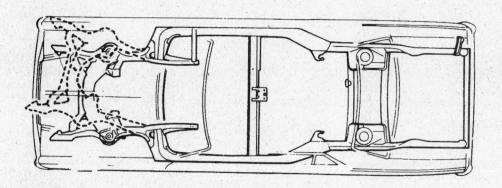

A side-impact hit can also cause a twist in the frame, whether a true frame or a unit body with frame "channels"

On vehicles with a true frame, look at the frame rails - a front impact may leave the side rail bent as in the dotted line here

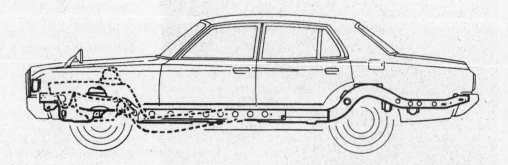

wheels on the right side are lined up with each other, the wheels on one side may be sticking out from the body more than the wheels on the other side. If they are, the vehicle has been hit.

Here's another way to check for a bent frame: Squatting alongside a front wheel, look at the space *behind* the wheel, i.e. the space between the rear of the wheel and the trailing edge of the wheel housing or wheel well. Pull out your six-inch ruler and measure this distance. Now go to the other front wheel and measure the distance between the rear of that wheel and the rear of the wheel housing. The distance should be approximately the same as the other front wheel. Measure this same gap at the rear wheels. If you discover that the distance

This unit body design illustrates the strengthening ribs stamped into the floorpan in unit body construction - if you look underneath, look for these to be straight and free of non-factory welds

If you find any signs of mismatched paint, overspray, etc. sight along the sides of the car in strong outdoor light and look for wavy or mismatched door, fender and quarter panels. Wavy panels usually indicate poor bodywork; mismatched panels usually point to a frame that's been tweaked to the point that things no longer line up

Squat down about 10 to 15 feet behind the car and sight along each side to verify that the front and rear wheels are lined up on both sides of the vehicle. If they're not lined up, the vehicle has been in an accident (repeat this procedure from the front of the car as well)

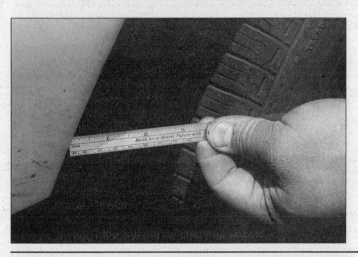

Measure the distance between the rear of each wheel and the rear edge of the wheel housing or wheel well. This distance should be the same for the two front wheels and the two rear wheels; if it isn't, the car has been hit

Look to see if the relationship of the tire to the body gap around it is the same on both sides of the car - you can often use your fingers or hand as an impromptu ruler for a quick check

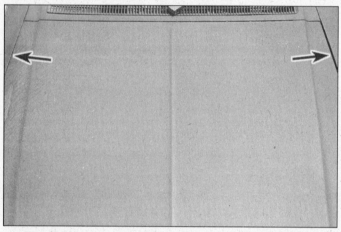

Check the gaps between the hood and the front fender panels, then check the gap between the trunk lid and the rear quarter panels

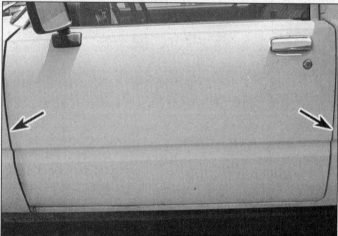

Check the gaps between the doors and the body; they should be the same width all the way around. If they're not, either the door or an adjacent body panel is misaligned

Tip

A seriously bent frame will also be noticeable as you drive the car. Uneven steering, instability, screeching tires while driving straight, "rolling" after driving over a bump and uneven tire wear are all symptoms. These symptoms can be caused by worn steering/suspension parts or poor front or rear wheel alignment, but, when combined with evidence of a wreck, these symptoms are strong reasons to suspect a bent frame.

This is how the right end of a typical upper radiator crossmember is welded to the gusset which is part of the inner fender panel; notice how clean and neat the spot welds are

between a left front or left rear wheel and its wheel housing is vastly different from the corresponding distance at the right front or rear wheel, the frame or unit body is bent.

If the frame seems to be straight and the wheels are aligned, the car probably hasn't been in a bad accident. But has it been in a less serious one, a fender bender? Open and close all the doors, the hood and the trunk. Make sure they fit properly. The gaps between the doors and the body should be equal all the way around. Ditto for the hood and trunk. A large gap on one side and a smaller gap on the other side means either that new body panels have been installed or the old ones have been removed and refinished, then reinstalled. Either way, the vehicle was probably involved in an accident.

Another way to spot damage is to look for signs of non-factory welds. If a vehicle is involved in a head-on collision, the upper and lower radiator crossmembers are usually damaged. In the accompanying photos, note how the left upper crossmember has been re-welded to the front fenders.

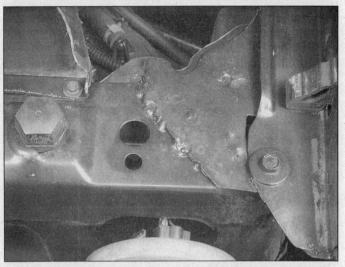

Now look at the left end of the crossmember: The welds are sloppy, the gusset is distorted and the distance between the gusset and the larger hole in the crossmember is greater than the distance between the gusset and the hole in the previous photo. This car has had front end damage

Rust never sleeps

Rust is an electrochemical process that corrodes ferrous metals (iron and steel) from the inside out. It's usually caused by the exposure of unprotected (uncoated) surfaces to air and moisture. Rust can occur anywhere that humidity, industrial pollution or chemical salts are present. Coastal areas, with their high humidity and salt air, are an ideal environment for accelerating the ravages of rust. In colder climates, the problem is the chemical salt (de-icer) that's used to keep the roads clear. And in industrial areas plagued by sulfur dioxide emissions, the sulfur dioxide turns to sulfuric acid when it rains. The rusting process is also accelerated by high temperatures. For example, the underside of a vehicle that is driven over slushy roads in a snowy area should be hosed off at the end of the day, but is often left overnight in a heated garage instead. After several months of this type of neglect, a car's exposed metal surfaces are doomed.

Automotive design and manufacturing techniques also contribute to rust formation: Spot welded panels produce small pockets that trap moisture and provide a perfect environment for rust formation. Auto manufacturers have been working hard to increase the corrosion protection of their products. Galvanized sheet metal is used widely nowadays; so are various rust-retardant coatings. Manufacturers are also designing-out areas in the body where rust-forming moisture can collect. Plastic body panels are becoming more widely used by the major manufacturers. Several vehicles on the road today are constructed mostly, if not entirely of plastic body panels. Bumper covers and side rocker moldings are commonly made of plastic. They offer the vehicle a certain amount of protection against dents and dings, since the plastic can withstand a slight impact without denting; and of course plastic will not rust or corrode.

If you find surface rust on the underside of the pan, look inside - you'll probably find that water trapped between the carpeting and the pan has eaten its way through the floor; this particular example is also a "clip" - note the welded junction between the original pan (below) and the newer pan (above)

> ## Tip
> If you live in a rust-prone area, be sure to rustproof your vehicle after purchase. Details are in the *Haynes Automotive Detailing Manual*.

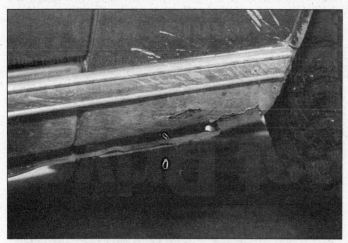

Bubbles on the rocker panel are a sure sign of advanced body rot below the doors

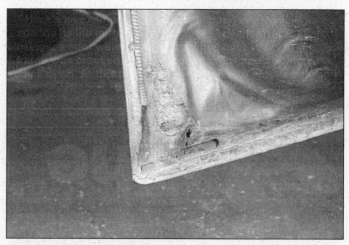

2.49 Rust in the lower parts of the door means that water has entered the door and is sitting at the bottom, eating its way out; doors are supposed to drain and dry out after a rain or a car wash, but drain holes in the doors can become clogged by leaves or dirt

Get back on the ground and look for signs of rust on the car's pan and/or frame. If you see pockets of rust beginning to form on the pan, water damage from above, i.e. from within the car, has done its work. The pan has been seriously compromised.

Here are some other places to look for rust:

a) Look for bubbles on the "rocker panels" (the sheet metal beneath the doors and between the wheels) and along all other lower body panels on each side of the car. Bubbles are an indicator of serious body rot, where rust has eaten its way through the metal from the inside out. Even if bubbling doesn't negate the sale, you'll want to get a hefty discount for this one.

b) Look for rust spots or bubbles along the bottom edges

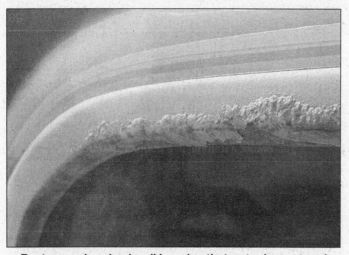

Rust around a wheel well is a sign that water has entered body voids in front of, above or behind the wheel well, then eaten its way through the fender panel

Rust forms below the windshield when water seeps through an old, cracked window molding, gets into the cavity below the molding and sits there until it eats it way out

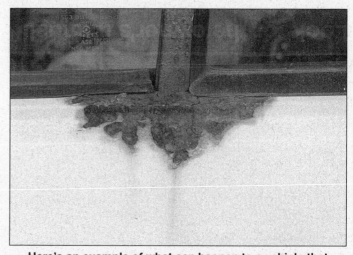

Here's an example of what can happen to a vehicle that spends its life in the salt air near the ocean: After repeated closings, a spot weld that attached this door panel to the door frame was cracked, weakening the panel and allowing it to crack open. At this point, water was able to enter easily and the salt air did the rest

Here's what the area at the back of the rear window looks like on the same vehicle: Water seeped past the window molding into a void below the window until it could eat its way through

The "A-pillar" (the pillar between the windshield and the front door) can become rusted out when water gets past the windshield molding, seeps along the molding to the pillar, then drips down into the pillar, where it sits until it eats it way to daylight - this damage is very expensive to repair

of the doors. Water seeps past the window seals and trickles down into the door voids, where it sits silently until it eats its way out the bottom of the door. Depending on the overall value of the vehicle, this type of damage might be affordable to repair, if you're willing to track down a door from a salvaged vehicle and simply swap doors. Otherwise, forget it. Repairing a door is expensive.

c) Look for rust damage around the wheel wells. Water that gets into the body sometimes finds it way into voids in front of, above and below the wheel wells. There is no way for water to drain from these voids or evaporate, so it sits.

d) Look for rust spots around the front windshield, the side windows, and the rear window, usually along the

bottom edges. As the window/windshield molding ages, it dries out and cracks. Water enters gaps between the window and molding, or simply goes right through cracks in the molding. Either way, the result is the same. The recess between the molding and the body rusts out. Once the rust appears on the exterior surface, the damage is done, and is very expensive to repair, since the rotted metal must be cut out and new metal welded in, which can only be done after the windshield or other adjoining glass is removed.

e) Look for signs of rust on the "pillars" (the vertical stanchions that support the roof in front of, between and behind the doors). The bottoms of the pillars are a favorite breeding ground for rust. Water gets in through a

When you find rust in the vicinity of the B-pillar (the pillar between the front door and the rear quarter panel, or between the front and rear doors) and both doors, as shown, the rust has spread everywhere

Rainwater in the roof rain gutters has eaten into this roof and the C-pillar (the pillar between the side window and the rear window, or between the rear door and the side window or rear window)

gap in the window molding, then trickles down the pillar where it sits until it eats its way through. Because windshield moldings invariably leak at the gap in their molding, the A-pillars (the front pillars) are particularly susceptible to this type of rust damage. This type of damage is so expensive to repair that it may cost more to fix than the vehicle is worth.

f) Lift up the floor mats or carpeting inside the vehicle. Do they smell moldy? Are there signs of water damage or rust stains. Is there standing water underneath the mats or carpeting? If the water smells like antifreeze, the heater core may be leaking. Water from outside gets into the car's interior through holes in the firewall. There are holes for the brake and clutch pedal linkage rods, the accelerator cable, the shift cables, the heater core hoses, the air conditioning evaporator lines and the large wiring harnesses that connect the engine compartment to the wiring under the dash. These holes are usually insulated by rubber grommets which crack and dry out with age and sometimes fall out. Or they're incorrectly installed upon completion of some service procedure. A wet and/or rusted floor can also occur if

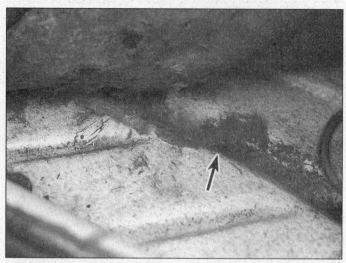

Lift up the carpeting and look for standing water, dampness and signs of rust damage to the floor

the vehicle has been flooded. In the case of flooding, look for the high-water mark on the trim panels. If it's halfway up the door trim panels, chances are the damage is more extensive, and more serious, than mere rust. The engine management computer, power window motors, power seat motors, shift lock systems and other electrical devices and systems are often located on the floor, in the console or in the kick panels in front of the front doors. If you find evidence of water damage from flooding, you'll need to inspect these devices, or have them checked out by your mechanic, before giving the car a clean bill of health. But the bottom line here is this: If you see any place(s) where the metal is rusted completely through the floor, take this into consideration before making your final decision to buy this car.

g) Look inside the trunk. Look for standing water or rust stains underneath the mats or carpets. They're often the result of a rear-ender that was never repaired properly or flood damage.

Tip

Rust is often repaired by replacing body panels or installing "patch" panels, i.e. partial panels that are welded into place. If you find evidence of panel replacement, make sure your search for rust is extra thorough and includes floor panels and frame.

Walk-around Inspection Checklist

Look for the owner's manual

- [ ] Owner's manual?
- [ ] Maintenance records?
- [ ] Federally-mandated extended emissions warranty?
- [ ] Extended maintenance or drivetrain warranty?
- [ ] Corrosion warranty?

General

Does the vehicle have a clear title?

- [ ] Yes [ ] No

Is the seller willing to allow a mechanic to inspect the car?

- [ ] Yes [ ] No

Body - general condition

- [ ] Good [ ] Fair [ ] Poor

Evidence of damage

- [ ] Yes [ ] No

Engine - general condition

- [ ] Good [ ] Fair [ ] Poor

Condition of the engine oil

- [ ] Good [ ] Fair [ ] Poor

Condition of the coolant

- [ ] Good [ ] Fair [ ] Poor

Exhaust smoke

- [ ] No smoke [ ] Blue smoke
- [ ] Black smoke [ ] White smoke

Fluid leaks

- [ ] Good [ ] Fair [ ] Poor

Engine noises or smells

- [ ] Good [ ] Fair [ ] Poor

Paint - general condition

- [ ] Good [ ] Fair [ ] Poor

Evidence of re-paint

- [ ] Yes [ ] No

Trim - general condition

- [ ] Good [ ] Fair [ ] Poor

Interior - general condition

- [ ] Good [ ] Fair [ ] Poor

Notes

_____

_____

_____

_____

_____

_____

_____

_____

_____

_____

_____

_____

_____

_____

_____

_____

_____

_____

_____

3 The Test Drive

Before you drive away, become familiar with the car

The test drive may well be the deciding factor for you in your initial assessment of a vehicle, you can tell here whether any further investigating needs to be done, but before you test drive the car, take a few moments to inspect the condition of the interior.

Look for the owner's manual

Is the owner's manual in the glovebox? This booklet is a handy quick reference for fluid capacities, belt sizes and other routine tune-up specifications. It also tells you where to find and how to operate all the controls and accessories, and the location of the spare tire, jack and lug wrench. On a loaded model, you'll need to refer to the owner's manual to learn how to activate and deactivate a vehicle security alarm system or an anti-theft system for the stereo, how to open or close a convertible top, how to remove and install a T-top, and any other procedures that may be somewhat involved. Don't play with controls whose function you don't understand. You don't want to break anything!

Most owner's manuals also either contain a section devoted to maintenance, or come with a separate maintenance booklet. When a routine service - say, the 30,000 mile tune-up - is performed, the service manager stamps

The owner's manual is a handy reference for:

1 Fluid levels
2 Routine maintenance intervals and procedures
3 Operation of all controls
4 Location of all fuses and relays
5 Location of the spare tire, jack and lug wrench
6 Warranty information
7 Emissions warranty information

Some owners - those who have their car serviced by a non-dealer garage or do their own maintenance, for example - don't use the factory manual or the factory maintenance booklet to record regularly scheduled services; instead, they stick invoices, work orders, receipts and other records into a folder and stash it somewhere like the glovebox. Be sure to dig out whatever you can find and go over it carefully

Check the odometer reading and compare it to the maintenance records from the glove compartment

Checking the odometer will bring you close to the steering wheel, so check it for signs of wear, stains, etc. that might indicate more mileage than indicated on the odometer

and signs the owner's manual. In the event of a warranty claim or a dispute between the owner and the manufacturer, these pre-printed records are used by dealers to determine whether a car has been properly maintained by the owner. Of course, some owners don't rely on dealers for vehicle service. They either have their car serviced by an independent garage, or they work on their own car. Owners who use non-dealer garages often stick whatever maintenance records they've got - work orders, parts invoices, receipts, etc. - in the owner's manual. Or they just shove this stuff into the glovebox. So don't overlook anything you find in there. A quick glance at the contents of the glovebox might tell you whether the car has been repaired after an accident, whether a major system or assembly has been repaired or replaced, whether the vehicle has been involved in a recall, etc. Or, the complete absence of any maintenance records might tell you that the car received very little maintenance.

But don't put too much faith in service records alone. A conscientious do-it-yourselfer may have changed the oil every 2,500 miles, the belts every 30,000 miles, etc. and have no records of any kind. But you won't have to take his word for it. This book will tell you whether he's telling the truth or not. On the other hand, some owners take a car to the dealer for all its regularly scheduled maintenance, and have it documented in their owner's manual to prove it, yet the car still may not seem all that well maintained, so don't use owner's manuals or receipts you may find as incontrovertible truth. Look at documented maintenance, or the lack of documented maintenance, as one piece of the puzzle. You'll find other important pieces in the next Chapter.

One final note about the maintenance portion of the owner's manual: This section also stipulates the maintenance intervals for whatever minor and major tune-ups are required to keep the vehicle in good shape (and in warranty). It's not unusual for a seller to unload a used car right before a major service, say the 60,000 or 90,000 mile tune-up. Look at the odometer reading. Now look at the regularly scheduled maintenance schedule in the owner's manual. Did the car just come due for a major service? Did the owner have it done, or do it himself? If it's time for a major tune-up, but there are no records to indicate that it has been performed, write this down and mention it to your mechanic. Have him give you an estimate of what the tune-up will cost and use this figure as a bargaining point when you reach the negotiation stage with the seller. If the service is already due, the seller should either pay for the tune-up before selling the car, or deduct the cost of the service from the asking price for the car.

Familiarize yourself with all controls before test driving a used car

Study the controls

Familiarize yourself with the location of all controls. Are they easy to find? Are they easy to reach? Do they do what they're supposed to do? Does the light switch turn on all the lights? Get out and check. Are the headlights, taillights and running lights all on? Have your friend, or the seller step on the brake pedal while you check the brake lights. Do both brake lights shine brightly? Activate the turn signal stalk both ways. Do the left and right turn signal lights flash on and off? Check the windshield wiper switch at all speeds.

Check all the power accessories. Try the air conditioner, heater and blower motor, defroster and fresh air registers. Turn on the radio. Try the volume control. Listen to several stations. Make sure the tuner section of the radio still works. Try the cassette and/or CD if equipped (as a courtesy, ask the owner's permission to try the cassette and/or CD player; if you're not using your own cassette/CD, make sure you handle his tapes/CDs carefully). Try the power door locks, power windows, power seat motors, power mirrors and any other power accessories which may be installed on the car. If anything doesn't work, or doesn't work like it should, be sure to jot it down in your notebook. You will want your mechanic to check out these items more closely to determine whether the fix is going to be cheap or expensive.

Try out all of the interior controls, such as heater, defroster, air-conditioning, radio and power mirror controls

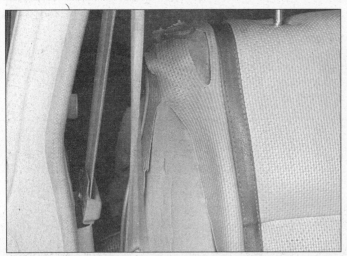

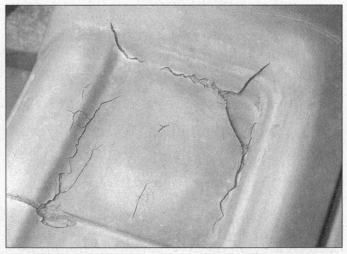

Since they can be recovered fairly inexpensively, ripped or torn seat covers aren't necessarily grounds for eliminating a used car from further consideration, at least if you are buying at the "well-used" end of the spectrum, but they're good ammunition for lowering its price during negotiations

A cracked dash has no real effect on the functionality or safety of a used car, but it's unsightly and expensive to replace (and it's also a sign that the car was left outside in hot weather, so look closely at other items that may have been damaged, such as weatherstripping, molding, plastic trim pieces and taillight lenses, etc.)

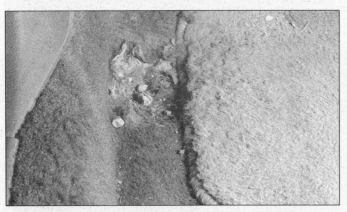

Although the carpeting in this vehicle is otherwise undamaged, the owner has planted her high heel shoe in this location for so long that it dug a hole in the carpet (which of course allows moisture carried into the vehicle by the sole of her shoe to find its way through the carpet where it can damage the floor pan)

If the speaker installations look like this, the speakers may or may not work, but you've got to wonder what the wiring harness under the dash looks like; owners who install speakers in the doors with duct tape may not be too picky about how they wire things together

A late-model car at the better end of the used-car scale should have a pristine interior with evidence of good owner care

Although sound isn't always an indication of a car's condition, you should listen carefully - leave the door and hood open while you idle and rev the engine and listen

Most engines today have sheetmetal shields (arrow) over the exhaust manifold - if it's loose, it can make an annoying tinny rattle - don't touch the shield to check for looseness unless it has cooled off

Inspect the interior

Give the interior a quick once-over: Look for torn upholstery; stains; dirty carpets; water stains; cracks in the dash from excessive heat and sunlight; damaged trim panels; scratched or cracked windows; tattered weatherstripping, etc. Don't get hung up on nit-picking the interior right now. You'll have more time for that later if, after road testing it, you're still interested.

Listen to the engine

Listen to the engine. Is it idling well, or is it running roughly? Do you have to pump the accelerator pedal to keep the engine from stalling? A rough idle isn't necessarily a serious repair problem; more likely, it's an indication that the engine needs a tune-up. Jot down your impressions and share them later with your mechanic. If you decide you want to buy the car, be sure to point out its poor state of tune during negotiations. The cost of a tune-up is definitely something you can deduct from the seller's asking price.

Is the engine shaking or vibrating? It is making pinging, rattling, knocking, grinding or squealing noises, or any other abnormal sounds? Are there any strange odors coming from the engine compartment? Is there a hissing sound coming from the engine compartment? Try to describe anything that feels, sounds or smells unusual. Some of these things - pinging or hissing sounds, for example - may be relatively unimportant, and may disappear after a tune-up. Often, a tinny, rattling sound may simply be a loose shield on the exhaust manifold or catalytic converter, something easily fixed. Others - such as a loud, low-frequency rumbling or knocking sound from the bottom end - usually indicates serious engine damage that can only be fixed by a complete rebuild. If you're only marginally interested in a vehicle, loud knocking sounds should disqualify the car from further consideration. If the car has no other problems, and you really like it, it's worth spending a few dollars for a couple of hours of your mechanic's time before you decide whether the car itself is worth buying. He could save you thousands.

Tip

Many engine noises go away or become less noticeable as the engine warms up. Usually, noises that go away are less serious, but make notes of all noises so a mechanic can investigate them completely.

Check the brakes

ALWAYS check the brakes *before* test driving a used car! Do the brake lights work? Make sure they do. Bear in mind that you could be ticketed while test driving a car with one or no brake lights. How does the brake pedal feel? It should go down no more than an inch or two, and it should feel firm, not spongy - even after you've held it down for half a minute. If the brake pedal feels spongy, there may be air in the lines, which means there may be a leak in the system somewhere. Test driving a vehicle with bad brakes

Try the emergency brake - it should take about five or six clicks to lock the rear wheels

It is very helpful to have a friend come along who can follow you in another car, watching for handling or for exhaust smoke going up a heavy grade like this one

could be dangerous. Don't do it! Insist that the seller fix the brakes before proceeding with your test drive or any further inspection.

Verify that the parking brake works and is strong enough to hold the car. Most parking brake levers should have to be pulled up no more than five or six clicks to hold the rear brakes. A parking brake lever that has to be pulled up farther than that is loose; a parking brake lever that can't be pulled up that many clicks may be too tight. Pedal-style parking-brake release mechanisms should also take about five or six clicks to apply the rear brakes. If a pedal-type parking brake system requires significantly less or more clicks than that to apply the brakes, make a note of it for your mechanic. We'll look at the brakes again as soon as you're underway.

Test driving the car

Never buy a car before driving it. If the owner or dealer balks, seriously question his motives. Sign nothing (it could be a sales contract!). And drive *carefully*. It's not your car yet! Drive slowly at first on city streets to get the "feel" of the car before heading for the highway. Get comfortable with the way the car steers and stops before driving it briskly. And take as much time as you need. If the owner or a salesman insists on accompanying you, don't let him distract you from the job at hand. Some savvy sellers will turn on the radio to mask funny engine noises that might discourage a buyer. You want to know about those funny noises. Turn off the radio until you've had time to listen for any noises coming from the engine or the rest of the car. During the test drive, stay focused. Pay attention. Concentrate! You may hear, smell or feel something in the next few minutes that could save you hundreds, even thousands, in repair bills (not to mention the purchase price of the car).

What friends are for

If you brought along a friend, have him or her follow you in another car during the test drive. Following from behind, a friend can:

a) Watch what comes out the tailpipe (black, blue or white smoke)
b) Verify whether the brake, running and turn signal lights all work properly
c) Verify whether the wheels wobble (if so, the wheels are out of balance)
d) Verify whether the front wheels are in line with the rear wheels (if not, frame is bent)
e) Verify whether the wheels bounce up and down constantly (if so, shocks are gone)
f) On convertibles, verify whether the top billows and ripples in the wind.

How are the ergonomics?

Ergonomics is the science of making work lighter, more efficient and more comfortable. In a car, the term refers to the design and positioning of the controls, the switches, the instruments, the seats, the pedals and the steering wheel so that they're ideally located for easy and comfortable operation and reading. Does the seating position feel comfortable and natural? Or does it feel awkward and uncomfortable? Move the seat forward or backward until you're positioned correctly. Sitting more or less vertically, with the seat back sloping slightly to the rear, you should be able to reach the steering wheel easily, with your elbows slightly bent and your hands positioned on the steering wheel at nine o'clock and three o'clock. You should also be able to reach the pedals easily. Make sure you can depress the accelerator, brake and clutch pedals without having to extend your legs fully. Finally, you should be able to reach all the

During the test drive, check the ergonomics (the relationship between the seat height, the seat back position, the steering wheel and the controls)

While in the driver's seat, check the operation of the door - does it open smoothly and stay firmly open when it should, and can you easily reach the armrest/handle?

important controls - headlight switch, dimmer switch, turn signal lever, windshield wiper lever, etc. - without taking your eyes off the road. A proper driving position is important. You're going to spend many, many hours in the saddle, so make sure you like the seating position.

If you're very short or very tall or very big, ergonomics becomes even more critical. Can you see over the wheel and the dash? Or do you feel your hair touching the headliner? On many cars, the steering wheel can be tilted up or down to accommodate the height and reach of different drivers. Adjust the steering wheel to a height that allows you to see the road ahead and provides a clear view of the instrument cluster.

On luxury cars, the driver's seat, and perhaps both front seats, may have motors that can raise or lower the seat height. If you have trouble operating the mechanical or power seat adjusters, or the steering wheel tilt feature, have the seller assist you. And if a power seat motor doesn't work, make a note of it. Of course, if you're simply too short or too tall for a car, no matter how you adjust the seat and steering wheel positions, consider another car. Don't bother road testing a vehicle that feels awkward or uncomfortable during a brief test drive. It will only feel worse on a longer drive

Don't forget about your passengers' comfort. The passengers' seating areas are an important consideration if you carry children or passengers in the back seat. Check the legroom and ease of entry.

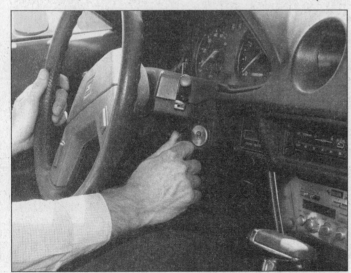

When trying the ignition key, see how firmly the key fits the switch - years of use with a heavy keychain full of keys may have made it sloppy and prematurely worn-out

Most of us get too excited to check out everything when seeing a car we're interested in, but stay calm and check out such subtleties as how easy/hard it is to get into the back seat

How's the view to the rear? Any blind spots?

Once you're comfortably seated, look at the rear-view mirror(s). Do they give you a clear unobstructed view to the rear? If not, adjust the mirrors. Many newer vehicles have power side mirrors. This is a good time to check out the adjustment mechanism, which is usually located on the left armrest, the dash or the center console. Rotate both mirrors through their full range of adjustment. If the power adjuster doesn't work, make a note of it. Once you've got the mirrors adjusted, look around. Note whether there are serious blind spots in any direction. If so, keep this in mind when making lane changes and turns. Of course, if any of these blind spots make you feel extremely uncomfortable or unsafe, maybe this isn't the model for you.

Interior noise

Is the car noisy inside? Does the noise level bother you? If so, think twice about this particular used car model. Generally speaking, noise levels decrease with the cost of the car. Economy cars are usually noisy; luxury cars are nearly always quiet. But in between the two extremes, there's simply no accounting for why some cars make more noise than others. Some engines are louder than others. Air-cooled motors, which are currently used only in some Porsches, but were once used in millions of VW Beetles, are louder than liquid-cooled engines. High-performance and hot-rodded street motors with aftermarket air cleaners and exhaust headers tend to be louder than stock engines. But even some smaller four-cylinder engines, especially high-performance motors with double-overhead cam, 16-valve heads, can be noisy when revved to their limit.

Aftermarket mufflers are sometimes louder than stock mufflers. And some used cars have exhaust leaks. Noise levels vary with the location of the leak. A leak at the exhaust manifold or anywhere upstream of the catalytic con-

verter and muffler will be louder than a downstream leak. If the noise level seems unnaturally loud, make a note of this for your mechanic.

Wind noise

Another problem is wind noise. Some cars are less aerodynamic - a *lot* less aerodynamic! - than others. Generally speaking, the less aerodynamic a vehicle, the louder the interior noise as the speed goes up. Some of this noise can be muffled with sound deadening material, but not all of it. And some manufacturers use more sound deadening material than others.

> **Tip**
>
> Excessive wind noise is often an indication that the door or window weatherstripping is deteriorated or damaged. Check the weatherstripping again when you return from the drive.

How are the brakes?

Apply the brakes firmly several times - they should grab evenly. If they pull the car to one side, make a note of it. A vehicle that pulls to one side when the brakes are applied modestly will be difficult to control in a panic stop. If the car doesn't pull to one side when the brakes are applied modestly, try hitting the brakes harder. There should be no squealing, vibration or swerving. If heavy braking produces any of these symptoms, make a note of it and have your mechanic inspect the brakes, steering and suspension, any one of which might be the culprit. If the brake pads or shoes making grating or squealing noises when they're applied, the brake pads or linings may be worn. Make a note for your mechanic to inspect the thickness of the brake pad and/or brake shoe linings.

The brake pedal, as indicated earlier, shouldn't feel spongy. If it does, there's air in the lines and/or a leak somewhere. If the brake pedal begins to feel spongy, terminate the test drive and return the car to the seller immediately. Have him fix the brakes before proceeding with the test drive or subsequent inspection. The brake pedal should not pulsate. A pulsating pedal usually indicates warped disc brake rotors. Pedal pulsation, however, does occur - and is normal - on vehicles equipped with ABS.

How's the steering?

Note whether the steering wheel shakes or pulls to one side when driving at highway speeds. A shaking or shud-

While driving, hold up your index fingers and observe them while traveling over rough roads or railroad tracks - do your fingers shake side-to-side?

If the suspension and alignment is in good shape, you should be able to remove your hands from the wheel without the car darting off - do this on a deserted road at moderate speeds

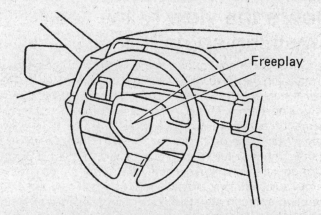

Freeplay in the steering wheel could indicate problems with parts of the steering linkage

> ### Tip
>
> Listen to the steering as you make turns. Power steering problems are also sometimes identifiable by groaning noises as the wheel is turned. It may be as simple as low fluid level, but you'll want to have a professional check it also.

dering steering wheel usually indicates a serious wheel imbalance or an alignment problem. If it's too severe, terminate the test drive and tell the seller to have the wheels balanced and/or aligned.

Take your hands off the wheel at about 35 mph. The car should still track straight and true, without veering sharply to one side. If it darts to either side, the wheels are out of alignment. Make a note of this for your mechanic.

Steering wheel freeplay (the distance the steering wheel is turned before the wheels themselves actually begin to turn) should be less than an inch; if there's more than an inch of freeplay, it could mean that the steering linkage is worn. On straight-aways, a tendency to wander from side to side or vague, unresponsive steering suggests worn components.

Does the steering wheel clunk or bind as you turn it? It shouldn't. Make a note of it. Is the steering wheel hard to turn? If so, the power steering pump, rack or gearbox may be wearing out. Power steering repairs - especially repairs to or replacement of a steering rack - can be fairly expen-

sive, so make sure you have your mechanic check it out.

If the car lacks power steering, can you handle U-turns and parallel parking without it? Power steering isn't all that necessary on subcompacts, but the heavier the vehicle, the more desirable it becomes.

How's the suspension?

Drive over smooth and rough pavement. Hit a few bumps. Drive over some railroad tracks. Find some expansion joints on the highway and run the car over them at your usual cruising speed. Excessive bouncing over bumps could indicate worn shocks, struts or springs. But keep in mind that, when assessing the ride quality of a used car during a test drive, you must do so in the context of the intended market for the vehicle which you're test driving. If you're looking for a firm ride in a full-size American luxury car, you'll be disappointed. Conversely, if you're looking for a plush ride in a used car, don't bother road testing compact sports cars. Generally speaking, the bigger and heavier the car, the softer and plusher the ride quality. The

Have your friend follow you to observe the action of the wheels, checking for excessive bounce or improper tracking

Don't look for a Lincoln ride in an Escort - generally the bigger the vehicle, the smoother the ride, but the bigger the car, the more the fuel consumption - every purchase is a compromise of some kind

smaller the car, the firmer the suspension. But there are exceptions. Some smaller American and Asian four-door sedans are designed and built for an older, more conservative buyer. These vehicles have a softer ride. And the suspension on some larger vehicles is calibrated toward the sporting end of the spectrum. Bottom line: If the ride quality isn't what you want, look elsewhere. Otherwise, you're looking at upgrading the suspension with all new shocks and/or struts, different stabilizer bars, etc.

Listen for any groaning or thumping noises from the front end that get louder or quieter when going around turns or over pavement irregularities. The struts or shock fasteners could be loose or the bushings could be worn out. Take some tight turns, some sharp curves: The car should feel stable and secure going around corners, without hiking up excessively on the inside wheels. If a car has excessive body roll in corners, the stabilizer bar bushings or the shock absorbers may be worn. Make a note of anything that sounds unusual or feels strange.

On FWD cars, clicking, clunking, rattling or ticking noises up front indicate worn CV joints. Usually, these noises are much more noticeable in a slow, sharp corner than they are any other time. Make a note of any noises of this type for your mechanic. CV joint repairs can be expensive, as much as a transmission overhaul or more to fix all four CV joints at the same time (although the outer joints are much more likely to be damaged than the inner ones).

A manual transmission should shift smoothly and decisively - accelerating through the gears is a good way to check the clutch and transmission

How's the transmission?

Run the transmission through all four or five forward gears (and don't forget to check Reverse). A manual transmission should shift easily without grinding gears. Some transaxles may lightly grind the lower gears the first couple of shifts on a cool day before the fluid warms up enough to allow the synchronizers to slide smoothly in and out of engagement. But if the gears grind every time you shift, either the clutch is defective or out of adjustment, the clutch hydraulic system is defective or, worse, the transmission itself has internal problems. A new or rebuilt transmission is an expensive proposition. Avoid a gear grinder!

The clutch should engage and disengage without grabbing or chattering, and it should be firmly engaged by the time it's three-fourths of the way up. Accelerate hard up to highway speeds and make sure the clutch is not slipping.

Is the transmission hard to shift in and out of gear? Sometimes this can be fixed by adjusting the linkage or replacing shift rod bushings, neither of which is an expensive repair. Sometimes it's a more expensive problem, like worn synchronizer rings inside the transmission. Try to define the problem and put it down on paper. You'll want your mechanic to look at any shifting problems. Some FWD cars use cables instead of rods to connect the shift lever to the transmission. These cables stretch over time and shifting becomes vague and imprecise. On some vehicles, such as those with cable-actuated shifters, shifting is vague and imprecise from the first day the vehicle was manufactured.

Shifting gears on such vehicles can be tricky. If you don't know whether the car you're looking at is equipped with shift rods or shift cables, ask your mechanic to look when he inspects the vehicle. And ask him to give you an estimate on any repair work that may be required.

An automatic transmission should also shift smoothly without jerking, slurring or hesitation. While cruising, accelerate sharply and make sure the downshift rod, or the throttle valve (TV) rod or cable, downshifts the transmission under acceleration. Electronic four-speeds have dispensed with any mechanical link between the throttle and the transmission; instead, the computer handles all shift points, including downshifts under a load. But they still must downshift during acceleration. After you've verified that the transmission shifts on its own satisfactorily, shift it manually. Make sure that it's actually in the gear indicated by the gear position indicator in the dash or on the shift lever console. If the transmission does anything that seems unusual to you, write it down in your notebook. Try to describe what the transmission is doing - shifting too soon, shifting too late, shifting harshly, mushy shifts, "hunting" back and forth between third and overdrive, etc.

Some automatic transmissions have more problems than others by design. You can find out which cars have troublesome transmissions by reading the ratings in **Consumer Reports**.

Tip

Ask your mechanic if the automatic transmission in the car you're having him check out is a basically sound design or a loser. Automatic transmissions are expensive to repair. You're better off looking at another car than buying someone else's transmission headache.

How's the engine?

Accelerate hard on a clear road - throttle response should be quick and sure. Back off and hit the gas again - there should be no "flat spots," hesitation or black smoke emissions. Does the engine "ping" under a load (accelerating, passing, going up a steep hill)? Maybe it simply needs higher octane gas. Or maybe it's a mechanical problem. Also, if the engine pings the knock sensor could be defective, or the ignition timing may be too advanced. Or, a buildup of carbon deposits inside the combustion chambers might be causing preignition or detonation. Listen for any unusual clanking or roaring noises coming from the engine when accelerating and when driving at steady highway speeds. Jot down any such noises in your notebook and point them out to your mechanic.

Note the gauges and warning lights. Watch the coolant temperature gauge while driving in stop and go traffic and note whether the car is running too hot. Low oil pressure or above-normal coolant temperature could indicate serious (and expensive) problems. An alternator light could be something simple like a loose alternator belt, or it could indicate a major electrical repair or replacement like the alternator or battery.

Pull over somewhere safe and stop. Turn the engine off, then restart it and note how well it starts when hot. Listen for any intermittent noises that you might have missed when the engine was cold. Check for leaks again. If the engine makes unusual noises, be prepared for problems. Insist that the seller has it tuned up or whatever it takes to get rid of the noise(s). If a tune-up is all it truly needs, he shouldn't mind doing it to sell the car.

After the test drive

If you haven't already done so, take a few moments at the end of your test drive to put your thoughts and impressions on paper. Don't leave anything out. These notes are vital to your mechanic. Even if you think a certain sound, smell or vibration might very well be nothing at all, write it down and try to describe it. Basically, a good mechanic already knows what to look for, but your notes will focus his attention on those potential problem areas you have noticed. When he does his own test drive and mechanical inspection, he will then either corroborate your comments and give you an estimate of how much it will cost to repair these things, or he'll tell you that a certain sound, smell or vibration is nothing to worry about.

If you suspect a serious mechanical problem at this point, you have these options:

a) Walk away
b) Buy the car and take your chances.
c) Have the problem checked out by a professional mechanic, who will tell you that:
d) The car is slightly flawed, but won't cost as much to fix as you feared; or
e) The car is seriously worn or damaged, or not as good as it looks.

But first, before taking the car to a professional, there are all kinds of things you can check out yourself, as we'll show you in the next Chapter.

Brakes

Are there any brake warning lights on?

☐ Yes ☐ No

Is there any brake noise?

☐ Yes ☐ No

Brake performance

☐ Good ☐ Fair ☐ Poor

Steering

Steering performance

☐ Good ☐ Fair ☐ Poor

Steering noises?

☐ Yes ☐ No

Suspension

Suspension performance

☐ Good ☐ Fair ☐ Poor

Suspension noises?

☐ Yes ☐ No

Engine

Engine performance

☐ Good ☐ Fair ☐ Poor

Engine noises?

☐ Yes ☐ No

Transmission

Automatic

Transmission performance

☐ Good ☐ Fair ☐ Poor

Transmission noises?

☐ Yes ☐ No

Manual

Transmission performance

☐ Good ☐ Fair ☐ Poor

Transmission noises?

☐ Yes ☐ No

Clutch performance

☐ Good ☐ Fair ☐ Poor

Controls

Easy to see, reach and use?

☐ Yes ☐ No

Interior

Windshield, door glass or back glass cracked, pitted or scratched?

☐ Yes ☐ No

Seat belts in good working order?

☐ Yes ☐ No

Condition of dashboard

☐ Good ☐ Fair ☐ Poor

Condition of interior trim panels

☐ Good ☐ Fair ☐ Poor

Condition of upholstery and carpet

☐ Good ☐ Fair ☐ Poor

Ergonomics

☐ Good ☐ Fair ☐ Poor

Headroom

☐ Good ☐ Fair ☐ Poor

Wind noise

☐ Good ☐ Fair ☐ Poor

The Haynes Used Car Buying Guide

Notes

4 Detailed Inspection

If the vehicle in question has passed your "five-minute" inspection and performed well during the road test, you are now back at the dealership or private party location and you're still interested enough to continue the examination. This time the inspection is going to be a little more thorough. You are now looking both for signs that indicate potential problems, as well as accumulating "points".

Points, for lack of a better term, are strikes against the vehicle. None of these points by themselves would be a big enough factor to keep you from purchasing the car, but added together and written in your notebook, can be used in your negotiation with the seller to adjust the price. The seller can choose to either have these points fixed or knock down the price (unless it was spectacularly low). He can bring the condition up to the point where you would be willing to pay the asking price, or if he isn't willing to deal with repairs, these points should add up to a reduction in the price, based on some ballpark estimate of what the potential repairs could cost (call a trusted shop for estimates).

Tip

It's best to wait until after a professional inspection before you negotiate a price – professional inspections often turn up problems you might miss.

For instance, if you find a small amount of brake fluid seepage around the brake master cylinder where it is mounted on the firewall (you can tell it's brake fluid that's leaking because it will wrinkle the paint on the firewall), this is not uncommon. It may have been simply the result of a sloppy job of topping off the cylinder, or the master cylinder is bad. Even in the latter case, replacement of most master cylinders is not difficult, and a new cylinder isn't terribly expensive. The potential need for a master cylinder replacement should become a bargaining chip for you. On the other hand, seeing similar leakage around the power steering lines of a power rack-and-pinion steering unit (such as is found on most front-wheel-drive cars) could be much more serious. The lines can be expensive to buy and to install if you're going to have your mechanic do the work, and if the rack-and-pinion itself is leaking, this is a serious repair that could cost $500 or more. If you spot a leak in this area, this is not a bargaining chip, it's a reason to pass up this particular vehicle.

Engine compartment inspection

Your preliminary, five-minute inspection should have told you enough about the condition of the car to have spotted any major defects. You know the car is fairly clean, and your subsequent test-drive should have further solidified your hunches about the vehicle. Now it's time to perform a more thorough inspection.

The Haynes Used Car Buying Guide

Most buyers of a used car want the same basic ideal purchase, a clean car that is mechanically-sound and in their price range. The first inspection of the body and interior has told you that the car is clean, and your second important consideration is mechanical condition. Thus, the first step in your more thorough inspection is the engine compartment. If there's one area that most used car buyers are concerned about, it's having a sound engine that will provide them years of good service.

Fluid leaks

If you are looking at a used car or truck at a new-car dealership or used-car lot, the chances are good that the vehicle's engine compartment has been professionally steam-cleaned and detailed. This doesn't mean that the dealer is necessarily hiding anything; he is just making the car as clean and "showable" as he can for quicker sales. Usually, the engine and engine compartment will look like brand

Most late-model engine compartments you'll see on car lots will look deceivingly new, since the dealers have most cars detailed professionally - finding evidence of lack of maintenance or high mileage will take some educated investigation

new. This has its good points and bad points for you as a potential buyer. New or serious, long-term leaks are easier to spot on a clean engine than a dirty one, and after your test-drive, any leaks that show up in the newly-cleaned en-

Fluid leak points on a typical rear-wheel drive vehicle (engine compartment)

1	Receiver/drier (refrigerant)
2	Heater hoses (coolant)
3	Thermostat gasket (coolant)
4	Fuel injection unit or carburetor (fuel)
5	Valve cover (engine oil)
6	Master cylinder and lines (brake fluid)

7	Water pump (coolant)
8	Windshield washer reservoir (washer fluid)
9	Coolant reservoir (coolant)
10	Power steering pump and hoses (power steering fluid)
11	Radiator (coolant)
12	Radiator hose (coolant)

**Fluid leak points on a typical
rear-wheel drive vehicle
(underside)**

1 Oil pan gasket
   (engine oil)
2 Crankshaft front oil
   seal (engine oil)
3 Fuel pump
   (carbureted engines)
   (fuel)
4 Fuel lines (fuel)
5 Oil filter (engine oil)
6 Transmission cooler
   lines (automatic
   transmission fluid)
7 Steering gear box
   and hoses (power
   steering fluid)
8 Transmission fluid
   pan (automatic
   transmission fluid)
9 Crankshaft rear oil
   seal (engine oil)
10 Cylinder block core
   plugs (coolant)

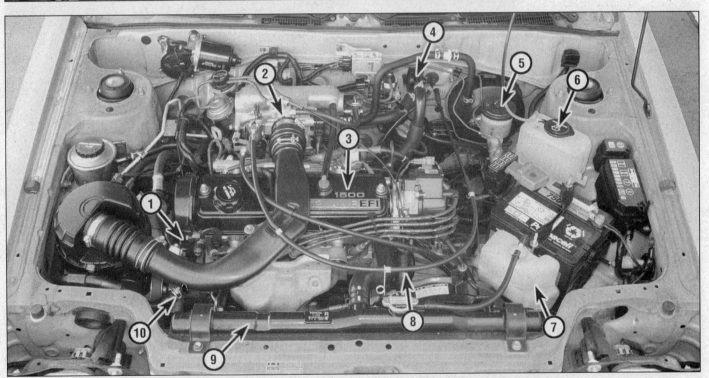

Fluid leak points on a typical front-wheel drive vehicle (engine compartment)

1	Water pump (coolant)	6	Windshield washer reservoir (washer fluid)
2	Fuel injection unit or carburetor (fuel)	7	Coolant reservoir (coolant)
3	Valve cover (engine oil)	8	Radiator hoses (coolant)
4	Heater hoses (coolant)	9	Radiator (coolant)
5	Master cylinder and lines (brake fluid)	10	Power steering pump and hoses (power steering fluid)

Fluid leak points on a typical front-wheel drive vehicle (underside)

1	Oil pan (engine oil)	5	Fuel lines (fuel)
2	Crankshaft rear oil seal (engine oil)	6	Driveaxle oil seal (automatic transmission fluid)
3	Transmission cooler lines (automatic transmission fluid)	7	Steering gear and hoses (power steering fluid)
4	Transmission oil pan (automatic transmission fluid)	8	Crankshaft front oil seal (engine oil)

gine compartment should be considered serious leaks.

The negative side is that the steam-cleaning has eradicated the "historical record" of the engine's performance. Small-but-constant seepage of fluids are much harder to detect now. Also, the rubber dressing that many detailers spray on an engine compartment for a "30-day shine" may make the underhood rubber and hoses look like new, even if they aren't. Our thorough inspection is designed to give

Dealers, and smart private-party sellers, have their engines professionally steam-cleaned, which removes the "leak record" of the vehicle history - if you buy a private-party car, it's a good idea to have the steam-cleaning done to make any leaks easier to detect

Take a look at the heater hoses, following them from the engine to the firewall

Looking up at the water pump from below (use a flashlight and a mirror if necessary) you may be able to see the water pump's "weep" hole (arrow) - if there are coolant stains present it means the pump is in need of replacement

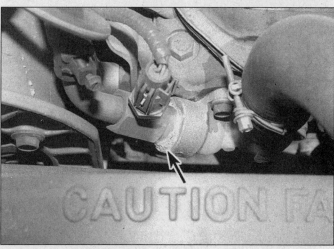

Corrosion (arrow) has begun here around the connection of this hose to the thermostat housing

you a more accurate picture of the engine's condition.

There are a variety of fluids in an automobile, including:

a) Oil
b) Gasoline
c) Coolant
d) Transmission fluid
e) Differential fluid
f) Power-steering fluid
g) Clutch/brake fluid
h) Windshield-washer fluid

Wherever there are fluids, there is the potential for leaks, leaks that have to be repaired. As explained in our example above, some leaks are easier to repair than others. If water is leaking from the coolant recovery tank, it doesn't require a major investment to fix, such plastic tanks are easy to install and relatively inexpensive to purchase if they need replacement.

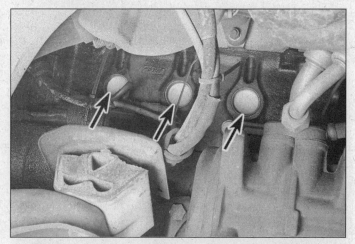

They are not always easily seen (this is shot through a fenderwell with the tire removed), but inspect the core plugs (arrows) on the engine - if any exhibit leaks, replacement labor can be very expensive

Tip

Rusted-out core plugs are an indication that the cooling system has been neglected. Regular cooling system servicing will prevent rusted core plugs.

What you do *not* want to find would be coolant leaks around the radiator, radiator hoses, water pump, heater hoses, bypass hose, thermostat housing or intake manifold. Most serious would be water that seems to be leaking from the engine itself, either from the cylinder-head-to-block juncture or from the basic block itself. The former would indicate leaking head gaskets, while the latter could be core plugs in the block that are rusting out. Replacing head gaskets is a fairly big job. Usually, there is enough work associated with removing the cylinder heads to replace the gaskets that a full valve job is generally done at the same time that the engine is disassembled for head gaskets. Core plugs (also erroneously called "freeze" plugs) are themselves very inexpensive, but often there is considerable labor involved in getting at them for replacement. We would recommend that if you discover any core plugs are leaking, pass the vehicle up. Such plugs generally rust out at the same rate, and if some are rusting out, the others aren't far behind. Even worse than the labor to get at the obvious plugs on a block are the hidden ones at the rear of the engine, which usually require transmission removal to replace.

Check the radiator tanks and core over very carefully, looking for discolorations or wet areas. All the fins in the core should be a uniform color. When you see an area of the core that exhibits light-green color (copper sulfate from

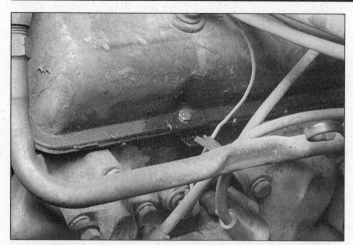

Oil leaks from valve covers are common on engines with 50,000 miles on them, but some models are labor-intensive to replace the gaskets

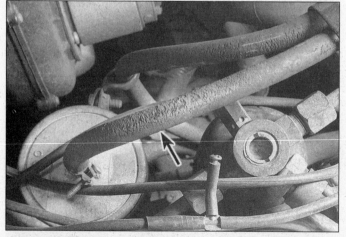

On carburetors or throttle bodies, try to wiggle the throttle shaft to check for wear, which can cause poor idling

corrosion), it indicates there is a pinhole leak in that area, and radiator repairs or replacements are expensive. Look at the bottom tank especially. If it's wet at all, try to see where the coolant has originated.

Look for oil leaks around the valve covers, on the oil pan (observe from underneath), around the oil filter and at the front of the engine behind the crankshaft pulley. Valve cover oil leaks are common on vehicles with more than 50,000 miles, and in most cases not too difficult or expensive to repair (by installing new valve cover gaskets). Some fuel-injected vehicles require considerable work to get at the valve covers for gasket replacement, so this would be a good item to note for consideration by your mechanic. In the same way, a new oil pan gasket set is inexpensive, but on some vehicles the labor to replace them isn't. Oil leaks around the crankshaft pulley up front indicate a leaking crankshaft oil seal, which requires some effort to replace as well. Oil leaks around the oil filter or oil pressure sending unit are generally easy to take care of.

Fuel leaks are uncommon and generally quite notice-able, particularly on modern, fuel-injected cars, which have high fuel system pressure that would cause any leaks to show up dramatically. Look for the residue of fuel stains on the intake manifold and look carefully at the fuel lines and hoses leading up to the carburetor or fuel injection unit. On carbureted engines, look at the fuel pump itself (usually mounted near the lower front of the engine) for signs of leakage around the fittings or past the gaskets. replacing the mechanical fuel pump on a carbureted vehicle is neither expensive or difficult, but on fuel-injected models, the high-pressure electric pump is expensive and usually located inside the fuel tank, making replacement more labor-intensive. On all models, be aware of any fuel smell under the hood or while driving. Any fuel smell generally indicates a leak.

On air-conditioned vehicles, look for any signs of refrigerant leakage around the hoses, compressor or fittings. If the air conditioning didn't blow cold-enough air when you tried it on your test-drive, check to see if there is a refrigerant sight-glass in the system. Looking at the sight glass

Inspect the fuel lines and other hoses carefully - this fuel line is deteriorating and should be replaced for safety

If the vehicle is equipped with a mechanical fuel pump (usually associated with a carbureted engine) inspect the fuel pump for signs of fuel leakage

Look at the sight glass (arrow) on the receiver/drier of the air-conditioning system - bubbles in the fluid while operating indicates the system is low on refrigerant

> ## Tip
>
> If the engine is greasy, look for "clean" areas around the fuel system components. Since fuel is a solvent for grease and oil, a clean area indicates a likely fuel leak area.

with the engine running and air conditioning on, the sight glass should be clear. The presence of bubbles indicates the system is low on refrigerant and needs recharging. If the vehicle proves out to otherwise meet all your criteria, ask the dealer to charge the system, and then you should check it out again.

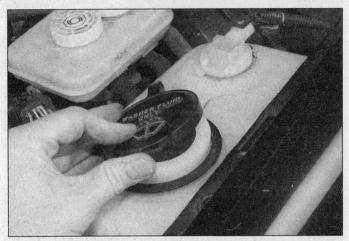

Make sure the windshield washer reservoir has water in it and test the system

The windshield-washer system isn't the kind of detail that will either make-or-break a deal for a car if it meets your needs, but make sure the washer reservoir has water in it. If it's empty, it could be a sign that the washer system is inoperative. If the salesman or car-owner tells you "the washer works, but just doesn't have water in it right now", *put* water in it now and then see if it really does work.

The power steering system (if the vehicle is so equipped) can be a common source of fluid leaks. Check the fluid lines all the way from the pump (and from the reservoir to the pump on cars that have these components separated) to the steering gearbox, looking closely for leaks around the fittings. Check the fluid level with the engine OFF and the wheels pointed straight ahead. The dipstick will have marks for FULL, ADD, HOT, and COLD, and the fluid should be at the mark appropriate for the temperature of the engine. There should be no foreign matter or dirt in the reservoir, and the fluid should look and smell exactly like new power steering or automatic-transmission fluid (no "burned toast" smell and red or clear).

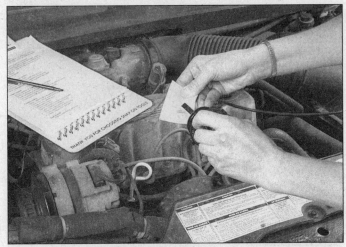

Check the power steering fluid level, and smear some on the back of a white card - it should be clear and clean

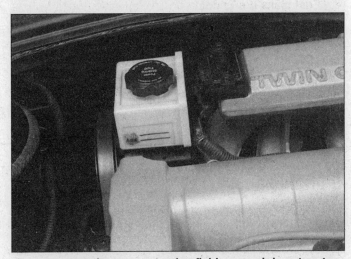

In some cars, the power steering fluid reservoir is not on top of the pump, but remote - this car has a translucent reservoir to make checking the fluid level easy

Inspect the radiator cap (do not remove from a hot engine!) for signs of corrosion - if the rubber gasket has grown larger in diameter than the metal behind it, the cap needs replacing

Run your finger carefully around the inside of the radiator cap neck, then check your finger for signs of rust or sludge-like deposits

In addition to looking for fluid leaks around the engine compartment, also check the level and *quality* of the various fluids. After the engine has cooled down sufficiently, remove the radiator cap and look at the bottom of the cap. **Caution:** *Do not remove the radiator cap while the system is hot and under pressure or serious burns and personal injury could result.* The cap should be free of rust deposits. Run your finger inside the neck of the radiator as far as you can to check for any rusty film that could indicate a cooling system that hasn't been regularly flushed or maintained. The color of the coolant should be green enough to indicate that it has the proper level of anti-freeze. Examine the coolant recovery tank. If the plastic is so obscured by rusty-water residue that you can't see the water level in the tank anymore, this may also signal that the cooling system hasn't been maintained.

> **Tip**
> Since coolant is a fairly good paint remover, look for signs of bare metal on the radiator and other components, which often indicate a leak in that area.

The coolant level in a coolant recovery tank will vary with the temperature of the engine. After your test drive, the coolant level in the tank should be at or near the FULL - HOT mark on the tank, and gradually recede to the FULL - COLD line as the engine cools down.

Automatic transmission repairs are very expensive, so examine the color and smell of the automatic transmission fluid. Pull out the transmission dipstick. The fluid should be clean and red, with no more odor than new transmission fluid. If it is brownish and smells burned (especially after the test-drive) this vehicle is headed for some expensive repairs. If there is a milkyness, it could indicate that coolant is getting into the transmission fluid, which is bad. The only way these fluids could mix would be an internal leak in the transmission-cooler portion of the radiator, which means the vehicle needs a new radiator at the least, and at the worst could need a new transmission as a result of coolant being circulated through the transmission. On a few late-model Japanese cars, the original anti-freeze is actually red in color, which can confuse the issue if you are trying to diagnose traces of coolant in your red transmission fluid, but the water content should still make the fluid murky if there is some transfer of fluids.

Engine oil can be an unsure indicator of the maintenance level. Chances are the dealer or private party has just

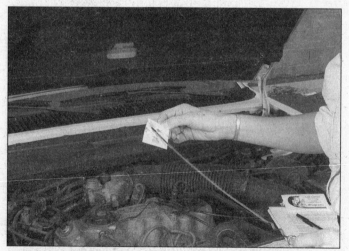

Check the transmission fluid dipstick with the engine running and the transmission in Park - wipe the stick on a white card and inspect the color and smell of the fluid

Remove the oil fill cap and inspect it for sludge or moisture, then look through the valve cover hole with a small flashlight and check for sludge inside, a sign of a high-mileage or neglected engine

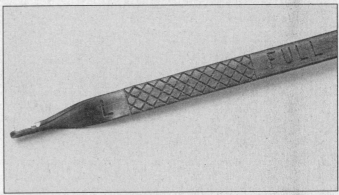

The oil level should be at or near the upper end of the cross-hatched area - you can make a close examination of the oil with a magnifying glass

changed the oil and filter before offering the car for sale, leaving the dipstick showing almost new/clear oil. A better indicator of oil-change frequency would be looking at the underside of the oil filler cap, checking for sludge or even condensation of water vapor, which could indicate a combustion leak (leaky head gasket or cracked head). If the oil appears thick and milky, it is usually an indication that coolant is somehow getting into the oil system, and this is a sure "black mark" against buying this vehicle.

Smell the oil, fresh or old, and check for the presence of a gasoline smell. This would indicate the car has been or is running too rich in its carburetion or fuel-injection. An engine ran this way for many miles will wear out long before it's time, due to the raw fuel washing the oil film off the cylinder walls. While you have it out, check the dipstick over carefully. If you use reading glasses, have them with you to make a close-up inspection, looking for any dirt or metallic particles showing, even above the normal oil level area. Check the *color* of the dipstick itself - If the engine has ever been seriously overheated, the dipstick can show a discoloration from the heat. Also pull out the PCV valve from the valve cover and shake it - it should rattle easily. A PCV valve that is full of sludge and doesn't rattle freely indicates an engine whose oil and filter haven't been changed frequently enough, as well as indicating the engine needs a new PCV valve.

If you suspect the engine may have a blown head gasket or cracked cylinder head or block (indicated by steam coming from the exhaust pipes, even after a thorough warm-up and test-drive), most radiator shops can perform a simple, one-minute test of the cooling system that tests for the presence of combustion gasses in the coolant. If anything shows up on this test (usually a fluid that changes color), you should have serious second thoughts about the vehicle, since there's a cracked engine block or head or blown cylinder head gasket.

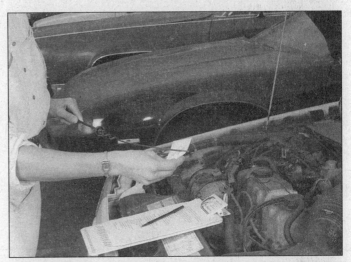

The white back of an uncoated business card is perfect to smear the dipstick oil on to check the color and quality of the engine oil

If the engine has one, pull the PCV valve from the valve cover and shake it - if it doesn't rattle it needs replacing and may indicate poor maintenance

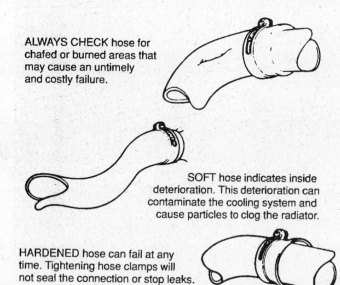

ALWAYS CHECK hose for chafed or burned areas that may cause an untimely and costly failure.

SOFT hose indicates inside deterioration. This deterioration can contaminate the cooling system and cause particles to clog the radiator.

HARDENED hose can fail at any time. Tightening hose clamps will not seal the connection or stop leaks.

SWOLLEN hose or oil soaked ends indicate danger and possible failure from oil or grease contamination. Squeeze the hose to locate cracks and breaks that cause leaks.

Check the cooling system hoses for resilience, cracking, swelling, soft spots or bad clamps

Inspect the vacuum hoses for cracks, brittleness and obvious signs of disconnected hoses

Cracks in a vacuum hose such as this one can lead to improper idling

Hoses, belts and wiring

The protectant spray that the detailers may have used will have left all hoses and wiring looking externally shiny and new, but could disguise any parts that may need replacement. Squeeze the radiator and heater hoses and feel for cracking or brittleness. Look carefully at the ends of hoses, where they are clamped. Swelling just "upstream" of the clamps, splits and swelling on the hose ends past the clamps, and signs of accumulated corrosion (especially where the hose attaches to the water pump, thermostat housings or intake manifolds) and all indicators of hoses needing replacement. Modern heater and radiator hoses are made better than ever, usually lasting up to 50,000 miles on older vehicles and as much as 100,000 miles on newer vehicles, but they have become more expensive. Thus, a vehicle needing all new hoses definitely gives you a mark for your bargaining list. Good hoses are insurance against future cooling problems, and if one hose has deteriorated, **all** hoses should be replaced, so your mental estimate of what this "mark" is worth should include the total job.

Besides the obvious coolant hoses, a modern engine has a myriad of smaller hoses related to the engine management system. There are small-diameter rubber hoses seemingly running everywhere, connected to vacuum sources, heater/air conditioning controls, emissions equipment, cruise controls, thermostatic valves and switches and many other components. You don't need a factory hose "map" to examine these hoses, just look for obvious problems.

Check the condition of the vacuum hoses first, by squeezing them with your fingers. They should be flexible, not hard and brittle. All such hoses will harden with age, making them prone to cracking and leaking, which can cause any number of driveability and emissions problems on late-model vehicles. Many of the vacuum hoses will be connected to each other with a variety of plastic "tees" or fittings. These also harden with age and can snap easily when you are working on an engine or even just examining it. If any plastic tee or fitting breaks or cracks while you are examining it, this is another bargaining chip for you. As with coolant hoses, these vacuum lines all deteriorate at roughly

It isn't much of a problem with newer vehicles, but on older ones look for non-stock wiring, bad wires shorting to ground (arrow) or . . .

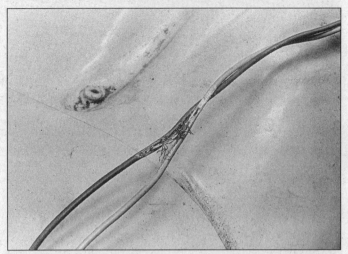

. . . frayed or abraded wires shorting each other out

> ## Tip
>
>
>
> If you're not sure whether vacuum hoses are routed properly, check the Vehicle Emissions Control Information label in the engine compartment. It should have a diagram showing proper routing.

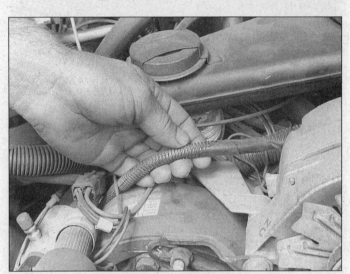

Check factory harnesses for melted areas, sloppy electrical taping, or wires pulled out

the same rate, so if one is hard or cracked, they should all be replaced. This is also a job that should be done at the dealership, because of the complexity of the hose routing on many vehicles (usually requires a large factory shop manual to trace them), and this should be done *before* the vehicle is smog-tested, if that is a factor in your state. Something as simple as a bad vacuum hose or misplaced connection could cause the vehicle to fail the smog-test and become unregisterable unless repaired.

While you are looking at the vacuum hoses, pay attention to how they are routed. Are they neatly arranged in what appears to be a factory original manner? Are there hoses that have been obviously pulled off of a component and plugged or pinched off? This could indicate work by an unqualified mechanic and may disguise some system or component that isn't working.

You can't tell much about the age or condition of wiring in the engine compartment, but look them over carefully nonetheless. Wiring harnesses should be good for the life of the vehicle, barring any tampering, accidents or ham-fisted mechanics. The signs to look for in engine compartment wiring are frayed or bare wires, missing harness coverings (loose wires out of the covers), wire harnesses not secured in factory clips against the fenderwell or engine, wires with

obviously-non-stock electrical tape wrapped around them, and added on wires that bypass original harnesses. Tape or extra wires added-in may signal a previous wiring problem, or an amateur installation of some accessory such as a stereo, accessory driving or fog lights, CB radio or burglar alarm. When such accessories have been professionally installed, the wires are usually neatly routed and bundled, secured to original clips or harnesses, and using crimped solderless connectors without a lot of electrical tape.

Like hoses, modern accessory-drive belts last a long time, but can be expensive to replace as a group. Some vehicles have as many as three accessory belts, driving such items as the water pump, power-steering pump, air-conditioning, alternator and mechanical cooling fan. Other late-model vehicles may have what is called a "serpentine" belt system, in which one long, V-ribbed belt "snakes" around all these components and drives everything. Using a flashlight if necessary, inspect the exterior of the belts carefully, looking for cracks or separations of the belt plies. Both

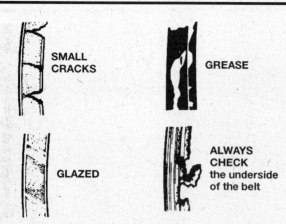

SMALL CRACKS

GLAZED

GREASE

ALWAYS CHECK the underside of the belt

Squealing noises, an undercharged battery or even overheating can be caused by worn, glazed or slipping belts - inspect them carefully

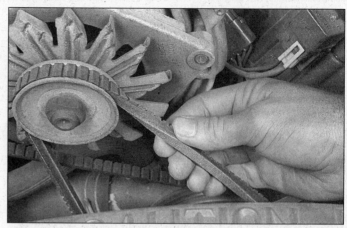

The "action" area of a belt is where it contacts the pulleys, so twist out the inside edge of the belt for inspection

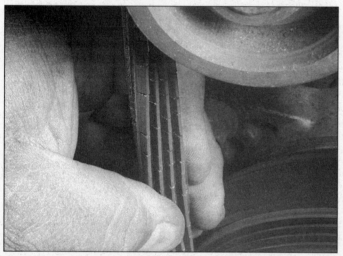

This serpentine V-ribbed belt exhibits some small cracks but . . .

CRACKS RUNNING ACROSS "V" PORTIONS OF BELT

ACCEPTABLE

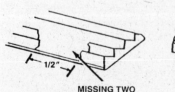

1/2"

MISSING TWO OR MORE ADJACENT RIBS 1/2" OR LONGER

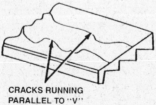

CRACKS RUNNING PARALLEL TO "V" PORTIONS OF BELT

UNACCEPTABLE

. . . lengthwise cracks or missing ribs are more serious signs that the belt is due for replacement

sides of each belt should be inspected, which means you will have to twist the inside edges out to examine them. On the inside of the belts, look for glazing, a shiny appearance that indicates the belt has been slipping.

A final check of the engine compartment should include a very thorough *listening*. Bring out the length of vacuum or fuel line hose you brought with you. The hose is used as a poor-man's stethoscope - you hold one end up to your ear and pass the other end close to areas of the engine where noises are likely to be heard (with the engine running, of course). **Warning:** *You must be careful to keep the hose away from rotating parts such as the cooling fan, alternator and drivebelts.* Areas to listen to for mechanical noises would include the water pump, timing chain area, oil pan (connecting-rod knock) and valve covers (tappet or rocker-arm noise). Also, move the hose end all around the intake manifold, carburetor or fuel injection flanges, listening for the whistling sound of a vacuum leak. Aim the hose around the exhaust manifolds to check for very small exhaust leaks.

Professional mechanics use a stethoscope just like a doctor to trace engine noises and find vacuum leaks - you can do the same thing with a length of rubber hose, just keep it away from hot or rotating components

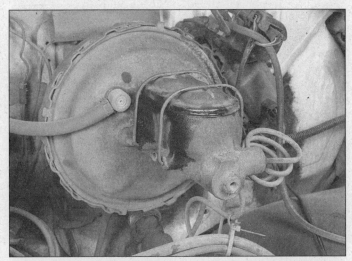

Some brake master cylinders have covers retained by wire bails that usually require a screwdriver or some other tool to open - this one exhibits signs (stains) of a leaking cover gasket or frequent refilling

Many modern vehicles have a translucent plastic reservoir on the brake master cylinder, making it easy to read the fluid level without removing the top

Engine compartment components

By this heading, we mean taking a close look at the various items in the engine compartment that we haven't already discussed, such as the engine accessories and whatever chassis components are easily inspected from under the hood.

The brake master cylinder, which is usually accessible on the firewall, should be inspected for stains and discoloration that could indicate brake problems. Either the master cylinder cap rubber gasket is leaking, or the stains are the result of constant topping-off to accommodate some brake fluid leak in the system, a dangerous situation. The fluid in the master cylinder should be quite clear, never murky, which would indicate a system with some corrosion in it, requiring a complete flush, refilling with fresh fluid and bleeding. On some cars, the master cylinder is a one-piece iron casting that incorporates the fluid chamber(s), while others may have a separate, white plastic fluid reservoir connected by hoses or a rubber seal to the hydraulic section. Checking the fluid level or condition on the former type requires that you use a screwdriver or other tool to lever off

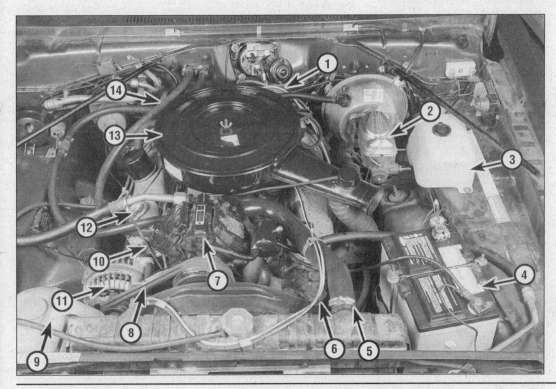

Typical engine compartment components - rear-wheel drive models

1 Spark plug wires
2 Brake fluid reservoir
3 Windshield washer reservoir
4 Battery
5 Radiator hose
6 Power steering fluid reservoir
7 Air conditioning compressor
8 Drivebelts
9 Coolant reservoir
10 Engine oil dipstick
11 Alternator
12 Engine oil filler cap
13 Air cleaner housing
14 Automatic transmission fluid dipstick

Typical engine compartment components - front-wheel drive model

1	Fuse block	6	Windshield washer fluid reservoir	11	Radiator hose
2	Battery	7	Power steering fluid reservoir	12	Radiator cap
3	Fuel filter	8	Spark plug	13	Distributor cap
4	Brake master cylinder reservoir	9	Engine oil dipstick	14	Spark plug wires
5	Clutch master cylinder reservoir	10	Engine oil filler cap	15	Engine coolant reservoir
				16	Air filter housing

the wire "bail" that secures the cover. Such covers should have a rubber boot inside - check its condition. On vehicles with the plastic-reservoir-type master cylinder, the fluid level and color is more obvious, and they have a simple screw-on plastic cap on top. With either type of master cylinder, check for the presence or dirt, foreign matter or droplets of water in and around the fluid, and of course check for the proper level of fluid. A low level could indicate that the brake linings or pads are well-worn - something to be checked into.

On most modern cars with a manual transmission, the clutch is operated hydraulically, which means that somewhere on the firewall (usually near the brake master cylinder) is a fluid reservoir for the clutch. It uses the same fluid as the brake master cylinder and should be examined for the same signs in the fluid.

Beyond just checking the brake fluid level in the master cylinder, remove the cap to check the clarity of the fluid

Tip

If the rubber boot under the master cylinder cover is badly deformed, suspect contaminated brake fluid. Petroleum-based liquids will attack and damage the rubber.

If you can see dark color when you drop some of the brake fluid on a white card, the fluid is old and/or contaminated and should be replaced

Many newer vehicles with manual transmissions have a hydraulic clutch system - its master cylinder (arrow) should be near the brake master cylinder

Examine the engine's exhaust manifold(s) for signs of cracks, leaks or stains. Stains could be from continual oil drips from a leaky valve cover gasket or other component, and cracks or blown-out exhaust gaskets could create dangerous exhaust-gas leaks. You can listen for sounds of an exhaust leak when the engine is running, or look for gray, white or black streaks on the cast-iron exhaust manifold. The streaks should lead you right to the crack or leaky gasket.

Brackets and adjusters for the various belt-driven engine accessories should be examined for any looseness, missing bolts, or cracks. Broken or loose brackets can cause accessories like the fan, power steering pump, water pump, alternator and air-conditioning compressor to not only lose belts but even fail before their time due to running misaligned.

If the vehicle you are examining is a front-wheel-drive car, then pay close attention to the boots on the CV (constant-velocity) joints. Most cars have an inner and outer CV joint on each side of the vehicle (left and right driveaxles), each of which is covered by a rubber boot. The CV joints are expensive to replace, and are packed with grease, and the rubber boots protect them from dirt, corrosion and moisture. Check the boots by hand by flexing or squeezing them to look for cracks or tears. A torn CV boot that has lost all of the grease from inside is a signal that the joints will need replacement shortly due to the invasion of dirt and moisture. Depending on the make and model of the vehicle, you may be able to check the CV boots from the engine compartment, otherwise, check what you can from above and do the other CV joints from underneath the vehicle.

If you're looking at a private-party car that hasn't been detailed, the condition of the car's battery may indicate what kind of maintenance the vehicle has been accustomed to. Often motorists pay no attention to a battery until the day it malfunctions and the vehicle is stranded somewhere. First look at the condition of the battery terminals and posts. Are they clean or covered with fuzzy corrosion?

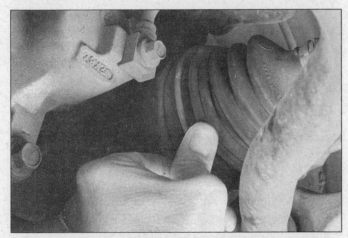

If from the engine compartment you can access any of the driveaxle boots on a front-wheel drive car, do so while checking the engine, otherwise do it during your under-car checks or ask your mechanic to check them

This situation on a battery post is a sign of maintenance neglect - an owner who routinely had the hood open for servicing and checking would have found and fixed this corrosion before it got this far

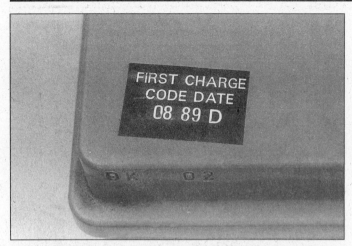

A battery can be dated by a sticker like this one or . . .

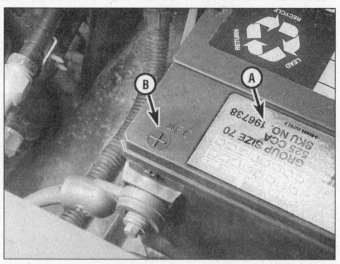

. . . one like this (A) with the dates punched out, or from the code stamped into the case (B)

Tip

Excessive battery acid and corrosion near the battery often indicate an overcharging condition. Have a mechanic check this out.

If the battery is not the original equipment battery, check the label. Usually mounted on top, the label has information on the date the battery was first sold, in the form of numbered dots that are punched out. One is punched out to indicate the year, and others indicate the month sold. By comparing the date it was sold to the number of months

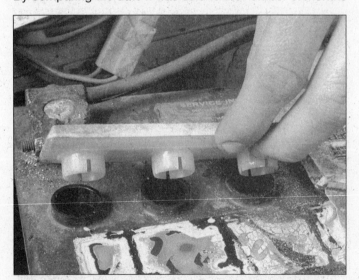

On conventional batteries, pry the cell covers off and check the electrolyte level - a really low level is another indication the vehicle's owner wasn't performing routine maintenance

of its advertised life will give you an exact idea of how much useful life the battery has left. A battery due to be replaced is another bargaining chip for you.

Look over the battery hold-downs and the battery box itself. Is there a battery hold-down at all and is it the original part? Batteries need to be securely mounted in the vehicle to prevent damage to the battery itself and to the engine compartment and nearby wiring, hoses, etc. If the original hold-down is missing, an aftermarket "universal" hold-down needs to be installed. Rope or bungee cords aren't enough to prevent vibration damage to the battery and potential acid spills.

The battery tray or box should be examined for signs of serious corrosion. Batteries that aren't maintained, where corrosion has been allowed to grow on the terminals and migrate down the hold-downs onto the vehicle's battery tray, can eventually become serious enough to cause the battery tray to disintegrate. The corrosion then attacks the unibody itself. If the battery is a type with removable cell covers (not a "maintenance-free" type), pull them out to see if the electrolyte level is up to the mark (usually a split ring inside). A battery with a low level could indicate either that it hasn't been maintained, or that the vehicle charging system is overcharging, something to note for your mechanic to test.

Many cars have electrical components in the engine compartment that you can visually examine. On the engine, look at the distributor cap for cracks or signs of carbon-tracking. Look at the spark plug wires - they should be clean, neatly-routed and free of cuts, abrasion spots or exhaust burns, and the same for the secondary wire from the distributor cap to the coil. Many cars have their main electrical-system relay boxes in the engine compartment, either near the battery or along the cowl/firewall area. Pop the plastic cover off the relay box and look inside. Usually the inside of the plastic cover has a diagram to indicate which relay is for which system. Don't be alarmed if there is a relay or two missing. Often manufacturers provide space and

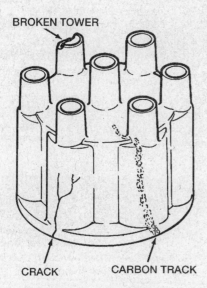

As part of checking the secondary side of the ignition system, inspect the distributor cap for outward signs of defects

Check the spark plug wires for signs of cracking, shorts or aging - this engine has three of one type of wire and one off-brand replacement - it needs a new matched set

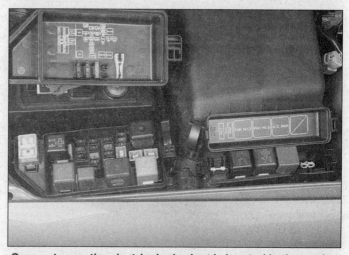

On most cars, the electrical relay box is located in the engine compartment - inspect the fuses and relays

wiring for relays that are only used on certain models or with certain options. If the car you are looking at doesn't have air conditioning, don't expect to see the air conditioning relay, but conversely, if it does have air conditioning and the relay is missing, it could indicate that there is a problem with the air conditioning harness, which someone postponed fixing by removing the relay.

During your initial inspection or test drive, did you actually turn on and try all the electrical components? If not, do so now. The air conditioning should blow cold air, the headlights should work on high and low-beam, turn signals should blink, etc.

Give the interior a second look

When you first looked at the vehicle in question, you may have been nervous or excited; this is a big purchase you're planning, and perhaps your initial examination of the interior was cursory enough to merely decide if you wanted to take a test drive. Now that you have made the initial "walk-around" inspection, have completed the test drive, and you're back examining it again, you should be relaxed enough to take a more critical look at the vehicle, including the interior.

If you haven't tried all of the interior appointments yet, do so now. Operate the wipers and the windshield washers. Do the wipers operate properly in all the modes? Try the cigarette lighter. Even if you don't smoke, the lighter socket is useful for a number of accessory items, and a non-working lighter socket may indicate some other electrical circuit

Try out the windshield washers to make sure they are working - also try the headlight and rear window washers if so equipped

Try the lighter even if you're not a smoker - the outlet has many accessory uses such as shavers, coolers, CB radios, etc.

If the vehicle has a remote door-lock system or car alarm, try it out

problem (or simply a blown fuse).

If the vehicle has power door locks, try them out. Make sure that all doors lock by trying to open them from outside (but don't lock the keys inside while trying!). At the same time, make sure that operating the door lock button really does unlock all the doors, again try them from outside. If the vehicle has a burglar alarm, set it and then see if bouncing the fender sets it off, but make sure you know how to disarm it before trying this. Some cars have a remote control for the power door locks as well, so try that out to see if it operates properly.

If you are looking at a convertible, you must try the top mechanism, even if it's a really cold day. There are complicated and expensive electrical and hydraulic components involved in a power-top mechanism and you need to know that they are working properly. Do the latches at the top edge of the windshield fit and latch securely? Does the top go all the way down and all the way up without hesitations or jerkiness? Make sure the vinyl boot cover (the snap-on cover that protects the top when it is folded down) is in the

> **Tip**
>
> Headliners are the least-noticed interior component, but become a real annoyance when hanging down on your head or in your face. Check headliners carefully.

car and that it is in good condition. Check all of the sewn seams on the top when it is up, and the condition of the plastic back window. Minor dulling or scratches can be polished out of the plastic, but replacement windows are expensive.

Try the radio or stereo. Hopefully you brought a known-

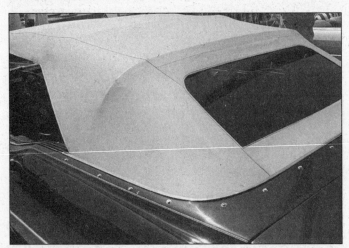

If you're shopping for convertibles, it goes without saying that the top should come in for close examination - look for tears, seams coming undone, stains and looseness

The biggest maintenance problem with convertible tops is the plastic rear window, they fade easily with outdoor exposure

Most convertibles have a vinyl boot cover that's installed when the top is folded down - make sure one comes with the vehicle and that its in good shape

Bring one of your own good cassettes or CDs to test out the stereo system

good cassette tape or CD (if applicable) with you to try the sound system. Most car systems sound OK with the car stationary and the engine off, but you should listen to the sound system and radio with the engine running, to check for interference from the engine electrical system or poor reception from a loose, broken or substandard antenna. Does this vehicle have a factory power antenna? If it does, it should go up and down either automatically when the key is turned, or when the ANTENNA button is pushed.

Check the seat adjustment for smoothness of the tracks. If it's a power seat, does it work, in all directions of adjustment? While you are in the seat, try adjusting the inside mirror for yourself, and check for looseness in the mirror mount that makes for a shaky image when the car is driven. If the outside mirrors are electric, try them out to be sure the motors/cables are working on both driver and passenger sides.

Try the operation of all the windows, make sure they all

> **Tip**
>
> While you're in the seat, notice the spring tension. Sagging seat springs indicate hard driving and high mileage.

go up and down, whether mechanical or electric. They should operate smoothly and quietly. With the windows up all the way, check the condition of all the glass, especially the windshield. Look for stone chips, cracks or other damage. Also check the operation and latching of the vent windows, if the car has them - a broken vent-window latch may indicate that the vehicle had been stolen at one time and may have suffered some damage by the thieves, such as cut wiring, broken ignition lock or disabled alarm system.

Check the positioning of the mirrors on the car to see if they suit you in the driver's seat, and try using the power mirrors if equipped

Small rock chips in the windshield aren't a problem unless they are right in your viewing area - they can be fixed at a good glass shop to be *almost* invisible

Here's a good example of aftermarket window tinting film gone bad, but most film-applied tints can be easily removed or replaced

Regardless of the weather, turn on the rear window defroster and feel the back glass to see if its operating

If the vehicle has a sunroof, open it and carefully examine the tracks and weatherstripping for sings of wear or leakage

Are the windows tinted? If they are fairly dark, chances are the tinting is aftermarket, and in some states could be illegal. Check your local laws on visibility to be sure you aren't buying a ticketable problem. If it is aftermarket tinting, It's usually a film applied to your original glass. If so, make sure it is free of wrinkles, tears and bubbles.

If the rear window has a factory defroster, try it out. Even if there's no frost to clear up, a few minutes after turning on the rear defroster, the glass should be warm to the touch if the system is working properly. Also check the heater (even if it's summer) and make sure the fan-speed switch works at all speeds. Try the windshield defrost position and feel for warm air at the base of the windshield. If there isn't any, it could mean that the defroster ducting is missing or broken.

T-tops are notorious for water leaks - open each side and look carefully at the weatherstripping

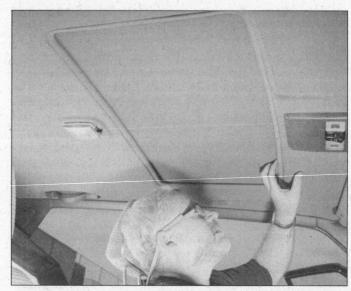

When inspecting a sunroof, check the interior side carefully - if there have been any water leaks there will be stains on the headliner or windlace

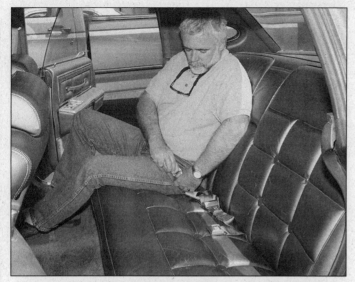

Make sure all of the vehicle's seat belts are there and that they work (latch securely), even in the rear seat

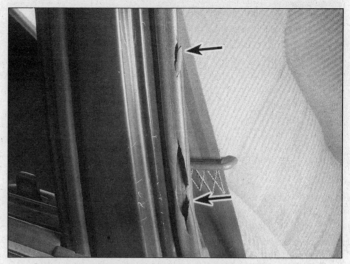

Open every door (and trunk or hatch) and examine the weatherstripping - defects like these (arrows) can lead to leaks or wind noises

Inspect the operation and condition of the sunroof, if the vehicle has one. If it is a powered sunroof, operate it to see how smoothly it works and if it seals properly when closed. When the sunroof is open, examine the tracks for any signs of water leaks, a typical problem with sunroofs, especially aftermarket models. If it has a glass or plastic panel, is it clear and free of cracks? Most sunroofs with clear panels have a sunshade panel that slides or cranks forward to cover the sunroof inside when you don't want the sun beating in. Make sure the shade is in good shape and operates properly.

Examine the seats for signs of wear, stains or damage, even try out the rear seat. Make sure all of the proper number of seat belts are in place and working - some people who still stubbornly refuse to use them may have the belts stuffed down in the cushions, particularly in the back seat. Do all of the belts click together securely?

You already examined the carpeting in your preliminary inspection, but now you can get down on your hands and knees for a closer look. See what's under the seats, look at the condition of the doorsill cover plates, examine the pedal pads, and aim your flashlight up under the dash. What you are looking for are signs of how the car was cared for and how much true mileage it appears to have on it. Worn pedal pads usually indicate a lot of mileage, though some sellers realize this and put new pedal pads on to disguise the situation. Under the dash, you are looking for an original looking appearance of the components and wiring harnesses. If there's a mess of tangled wires, electrical tape and obviously-non-stock wires, it means an amateur has been under there for repairs or installation of accessories, typically a home-installed stereo. If so, be aware that some of this electrical work may have been jury-rigged and may have disabled some other circuit or overloaded an existing fuse. Look at the underdash area around the pedal assembly for signs of wetness that could indicate that either the clutch or brake master cylinders have been leaking.

While you have the doors open, check the jambs for lubrication and service records that may tell the frequency of maintenance

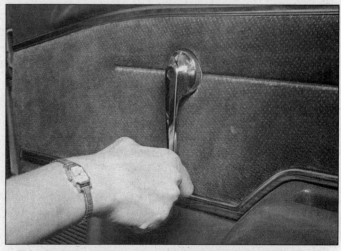

Try all of the window risers, electric or manual, feeling for roughness or jerkiness in the movement that might indicate problems with rollers or mechanisms

Check the dashboard heat/air ducting system by feeling for air flow at both the heater and air-conditioning vents

If you're lucky, you may find a sheaf of repair receipts and a maintenance record in the glove box, console or trunk

The original owner's manual can be very helpful in locating the fuel door release, trunk release, fuse panel, etc. and explaining their operation

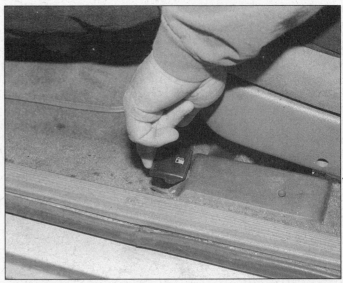

A remote fuel-door release is usually conveniently located next to the driver's seat; try it to ensure it works properly

An important final observation to make while checking out the interior is to look through the glove compartment and console (if equipped). There may be old receipts there that can tell you much about the vehicle's history, but you are really looking for a maintenance record. Most vehicles come with such a record when sold new, but many owners never bother to fill out any information after the warranty period is up. A used-car-hunter's "gold mine" is a car owned by the more meticulous-type person who kept a record of all service work, oil changes and maintenance, both during and after the warranty period. Chances are, the kind of a person who kept good records really took proper care of the vehicle. Be sure to ask if he has any additional records, since many owners keep servicing records in a separate file in their home.

Also look for the original owner's manual, which has a lot of good information about the operation of various items on the car, the fluid capacities and general specifications. Sometimes it's worth it to find the manual just to figure out how to set the dashboard electronic clock! If you find the manual, look up the factory-suggested maintenance schedule. If the factory suggest a major maintenance, check and tune-up at say 30,000 miles and 60,000 miles, compare this to the car's odometer reading. If the car is approaching one of these maintenance milestones and there is no record of the work having been done yet, the car is ready for service that will cost several hundred dollars, and this should be a bargaining chip for you. If it's at a dealership, get them to throw the servicing in with the deal. Also, if the dealership is the same make as the car you're looking at, this is in the perfect time to ask them to supply or order you a new owner's manual if one isn't in the car. Insist on it. Not only does it give you a lot of good information, but when you go to sell this vehicle, you have the right manual with it for the next buyer.

When you first open the trunk, check the operation of the decklid. Do the gas shocks support the weight of the decklid?

Trunk Inspection

Many people have purchased cars without ever opening the trunk. It seems like the last place to be concerned about, especially when you are somewhat excited about buying a new-to-you vehicle and there are more exciting things to check out, like the engine, stereo or paint job. However there are a few things to be learned from an examination of the trunk (or hinged compartments in the case of most station wagons).

First of all, and this seems like something too obvious to mention, but make sure there is a key for the trunk and that it works! Open the trunk and see how easily it operates. If it is a hatchback hatch, station-wagon back-door or glass, or the back door to a campershell (if you're looking at a pickup truck), make sure the gas-assist struts have sufficient strength to safely assist and hold open the glass, door or lid. It can be annoying and even dangerous to have weak gas struts that allow a trunk lid to come down on you just as you're loading something into the trunk. Some cars have a trunk release cable or electric switch inside the passenger compartment. Make sure this works, and opens the trunk or hatch with no problem.

Once inside the trunk, take a close look overall, checking for paint match. Is the trunk area painted the exact same color as the exterior, and does the bottom of the deck lid have the same color as it does on the outside? Very often when a car is repainted a different color, it is an expensive extra to have the trunk, bottom side of the hood, and the door jambs painted to match the new exterior color. Thus, a budget paint job doesn't include this work. Mismatches noticed in the trunk indicate either an inexpensive repaint or evidence of a quarter-panel replacement or some other collision repair. Look for overspray on things like the decklid hardware, floor mats, the cardboard panel behind the rear seat, the wiring or the back of the taillights.

Pull up the rubber floormats or carpeting in the trunk to look for rusting metal (not just rust stains from a picnic cooler that tipped over one time), signs of repairs and weld-

Trunk weatherstripping is important for the protection of items stored in the trunk and the trunk floor itself - this rubber has a torn spot that may leak water

While inspecting the trunk, check around the taillight wiring, looking for signs that a trailer harness has been wired in at one time

ing, or mildew that might be the result of leaking trunk weather-stripping. Examine the weather-stripping around the trunk opening, looking for breaks or deterioration in the rubber. Can you see the wiring that goes to the taillights? Look for signs like non-stock wiring or snap-on clips that indicate a trailer has been wired in. It could mean the vehicle was routinely overloaded. What about the wiring to the rear-seat speakers - does it look amateurish or professional?

> ### Tip
> Floor mats are sometimes used to cover up trunk floors that are rusted through. Remove the mat from the vehicle for a thorough inspection.

Look for the spare tire and original jack and lug wrench, especially if they are hidden under a panel - also look for floorpan rust

On some vehicles, usually trucks, the jack and lug wrench may be located in the engine compartment

Now look for the spare tire and check its condition, is it a tire you could trust if you had to? If you're buying what is supposed to be a low-mileage vehicle, the spare tire should be brand-new, and the same brand as came originally with the car, not a salvage yard wheel with a nearly-bald tire. Try to find the original factory jack, jack handle and hubcap/lugnut removal tool, they should all be there. Is there evidence of any flood damage inside the trunk? Check for the original jack stowage and usage instructions, which are usually printed on a decal applied under the decklid, on the trunk wall, or on a fiberboard panel over a spare if it's mounted in a recess in the trunk floor. The decal could be obscured, or missing as a result of some collision repair.

Most dealerships clean out the personal contents of

any car they put out on the lot, but if you are buying from a private party, check out any items remaining in the trunk; they may give you a clue to the service history of the car. For instance, if you see three or four cans of motor oil, a funnel, paper towels and two gallon jugs of water or antifreeze, chances are they are there because the owner was constantly adding these liquids to the car, so look more closely for coolant leaks, oil leaks, or smoke when the engine is operating.

Does the trunk have a courtesy light that comes on when the trunk or hatch is opened? Make sure that it works, too. Lastly, check the alignment of the trunk and the quality of its closure. It should close easily with one semi-firm push, you shouldn't have to slam it three times. When closed, see if the gap between deck lid/hatch and the rest of the body is even all the way around.

A final underside check

If you can see underneath the vehicle, there are a number of things you can examine. If you can't see well under the vehicle, make the best inspection you can and make notes for review by your mechanic, who will most likely put the car up on a hoist for a thorough examination.

A tight exhaust system is very important - not only does it make the car quieter and more pleasant to drive, but a leak in the system could prove fatal if carbon monoxide fumes get inside the car where the driver can breathe them. If you remember how the car sounded when you started it up before your test drive, you would have noticed any particular areas that sounded as if it might have a leak. If not, start the car up again briefly and have someone rev the engine a little while you crouch down alongside it (never get underneath the car while it is running, even if it is securely on jackstands). Listen carefully for any hissing or rumbling noises. Shut the car off and slide underneath for a closer

On trucks, you may have to look way underneath the bed to find and check the spare tire

When inspecting the exhaust system, look for signs of obvious exhaust leaks, such as the black stains around this improperly welded exhaust joint

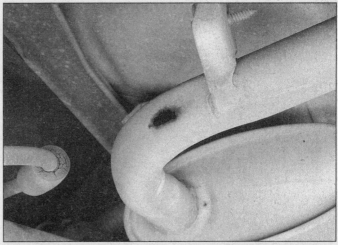

On light-colored exhaust pipes, leaks usually show up easily as brown or black stains - this stain around a small hole is indicative of a tailpipe needing replacement

look. **Warning:** *Never touch the hot exhaust system with any part of your body or clothing.*

Exhaust leaks usually show up as streaks of white, light gray or black. They may be coming from pinholes, cracks or holes in the exhaust pipes, catalytic converter or muffler. Look especially at muffler and converter seams, and joints where two pipes or exhaust components are joined. Wherever there are exhaust gaskets, there's a potential for exhaust leaks.

Observe all the hangers on the exhaust system. Are they all in place and do they all look like original parts? Most modern cars have exhaust mounts with a heat-resistant rubber "doughnut" connecting a frame bracket to a bracket on the exhaust. When these are replaced with universal metal straps at some muffler shops, the exhaust system will be under more stress and also transfer more exhaust noise, heat and vibration to the car.

If you do find defects in the exhaust system, have them taken care of immediately. The safety of you and your family isn't worth putting such work off simply because you just put all your ready money down as a deposit on the car. If there is a problem with the catalytic converter, you may not pass a state smog inspection anyway, so you won't be able to register the car in some states. Many East-Coast states have an annual or semiannual safety inspection, which a car will fail if it has any exhaust leaks.

The next area of inspection in your under-chassis check is looking for any fluid leaks. Start with the fuel system, tracing the course of the steel fuel line from the engine compartment all the way back to the fuel tank. Along the way, you should find a fuel filter, which you should look at to determine how old it looks. How dirty it looks compared to the chassis and components around it should tell you how recently it may have been changed. Most manufacturers recommend that fuel filters on modern, fuel-injected cars be changed at 30,000-mile intervals. If the one you are looking at is close to one of those mileage intervals and the filter looks just as dirty as the rest of the chassis, chances

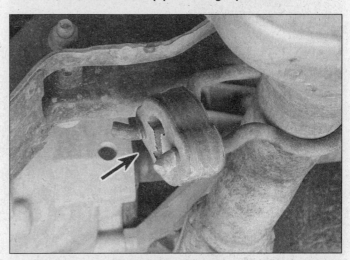

Check the condition of the rubber "doughnut" exhaust hangers, if equipped

It wasn't noticeable when driving, but a close examination of this car revealed a broken exhaust mount that could cause the system to leak or become noisy

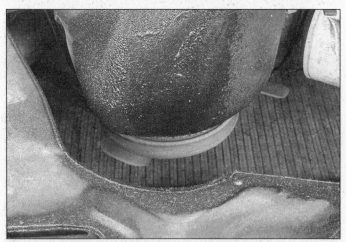

Among the kinds of things you can find when looking under a car are further evidence of something you noticed in your topside inspection - like this leak, which confirms the suspicion that the crankshaft front oil seal has been leaking

Some leaks are not a big deal, and won't make-or-break the car purchase, but a brake line or fitting leak such as this must be remedied immediately

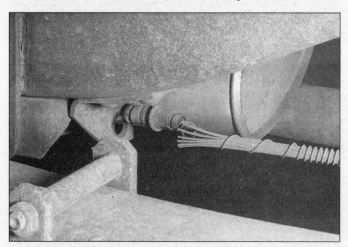

Problems with emergency-brake cables are rare, but check them - here's a cable that is frayed and the clip that holds it to the chassis is missing, so the emergency brake is non-functional

are it hasn't been changed, and you have another chip for your bargaining list.

Coolant leaks are generally most visible from above, but if the heater core or the hoses to it are leaking, the drips may only show up under the car, so look for such stains of coolant around the bellhousing/firewall area. **Note:** *Air-conditioned cars generally drip water, sometimes quite a bit, right after the car has been shut off when the air has been running for a while. When you have just returned from a test-drive and you were testing the air-conditioning on the drive, don't mistake such drops for coolant leaks. The water from the air-conditioner is condensation and will be clear and odorless, unlike coolant which should be greenish (anti-freeze color) and slightly sweet-smelling.*

Check the oil pan and oil pan drain plug area for signs of oil leakage. Minor stains are common on vehicles with more than 50,000 miles. When an oil leak has been going for a long time, the road draft and engine fan will have thrown the oil droplets all over the engine/transmission/lower firewall area, so serious leaks aren't hard to find unless the underside of the vehicle has been recently steam-cleaned. Frankly, most used-car buyers don't go to the trouble of a thorough examination such as we are de-

scribing here, so dealers generally don't pay any extra to steam-clean the chassis. They only clean up what shows when the hood is opened.

A power-steering fluid leak may look like a transmission fluid leak on some cars, because the fluid is similar, but generally the power-steering leaks will concentrate the resultant stains in close proximity to the power-steering pump or the steering box (or rack-and-pinion) itself. Look for transmission fluid leaks where the cooling lines are attached to the bottom of the radiator, look along the length cooling lines themselves, and all around the transmission pan and the transmission rear seal. The metal cooling lines should be routed in a pair back to the transmission, with several metal clips securing them along the way. The lines shouldn't be just hanging down. Also check that someone hasn't cut the metal lines at some point and installed rubber hoses with screw-clamps as a repair. Only a few types of rubber hose are strong enough and heat/oil-resistant

Tip

Road draft can easily obscure the point of leakage. If you're not sure whether it's an oil leak coming from the rear of the engine or a dirty transmission leak coming from the front of the transmission, let a professional decide.

Looking at this chassis, it wasn't hard to notice that this suspension bushing (left arrow) was cracked and long past its prime, and that the wet area on the shock absorber (right arrow) means all new shocks are needed

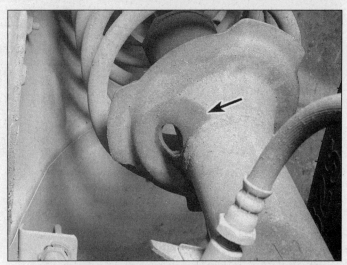

The hydraulic shock inside most strut assemblies is somewhat hidden from view when checking for leaks, but this shock's fluid has left a stain at this water drain hole (arrow) - the light color indicates the strut hasn't been leaking for too long

This shock has been leaking for a long time, and should have easily failed the shock absorber test in Chapter 3

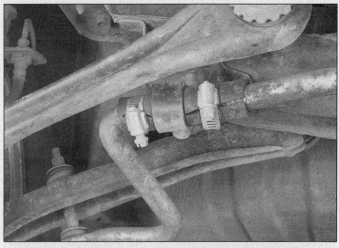

This is an indication of poor maintenance - a stabilizer bushing obviously failed and someone replaced it with a piece of split rubber hose and two screw-clamps

enough to serve as transmission fluid lines. Any regular hose such as fuel line hose can fail after a short life in this application, potentially causing transmission failure.

Still checking for leaks of any kind, examine the front and rear brakes for any signs of brake fluid. Look for stains on the calipers, drum-brake backing plates, and on the tires. Follow the steel brake lines from the front of the car to the rear, looking for kinks or dents in the lines or any signs of leakage. The flexible rubber lines that are attached to the calipers should look dry and free of kinks, cracks or cuts. If any exhaust system parts look non-stock, like replacement tailpipes, make sure they don't come too close to any brake lines. Where tailpipes go over the rear end on a rear-wheel-drive vehicle, make sure that the steel brake line that hugs the contours of the rear axle housing hasn't been flattened

by coming into contact with the exhaust on hard bumps.

The frame (or unibody structure) can be scrutinized better now than on your initial inspection because you have raised the vehicle where you can see under it. As we mentioned earlier, look for any signs of collision damage or repairs, such as wrinkled metal, cracks or non-stock-looking welds.

Check over the front and rear suspension systems. Up front look at the shocks, springs, struts, steering arms, tie-rod ends, stabilizer bars, control arms, balljoints and calipers. On some calipers you can see the amount of brake pad material remaining. Look at the backside of the wheel rims for any signs of damage from curbs, potholes or accidents. A wheel that is bent, even a little, may not hold air, may not be balanced, and may not run true. Driving

The Haynes Used Car Buying Guide

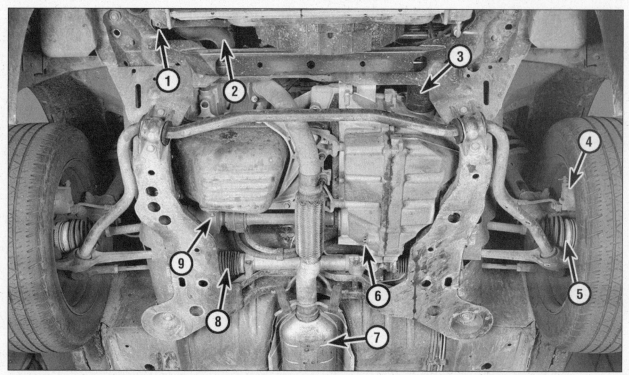

This is not a complete list, but here are some of things to check when looking at a front end from underneath:

1	Radiator drain location	4	Disc brake caliper	7	Exhaust system
2	Lower radiator hose	5	Driveaxle CV boot	8	Steering gear boot
3	Automatic transaxle	6	Transaxle drain plug	9	Engine oil pan

Typical view of a rear suspension system (FWD car) shows some of the areas to examine:

1	Fuel tank inlet hose	3	Disc brake caliper (or drum)	5	Rear suspension strut
2	Muffler	4	Fuel tank		

Condition	Probable cause	Corrective action	Condition	Probable cause	Corrective action
Shoulder wear	• Underinflation (both sides wear) • Incorrect wheel camber (one side wear) • Hard cornering • Lack of rotation	• Measure and adjust pressure. • Repair or replace axle and suspension parts. • Reduce speed. • Rotate tires.	Feathered edge **Toe wear**	• Incorrect toe	• Adjust toe-in.
Center wear	• Overinflation • Lack of rotation	• Measure and adjust pressure. • Rotate tires.	**Uneven wear**	• Incorrect camber or caster • Malfunctioning suspension • Unbalanced wheel • Out-of-round brake drum • Lack of rotation	• Repair or replace axle and suspension parts. • Repair or replace suspension parts. • Balance or replace. • Turn or replace. • Rotate tires.

This chart will help you determine the condition of a vehicle's tires, as well as the probable cause of improper wear patterns

down the road, even a tiny bit of runout can cause shimmy felt at the steering wheel.

On rear-wheel-drive cars, look the driveshaft over. A driveshaft that is bent even slightly or has a dent in it will probably induce an unpleasant vibration in the car and wear out U-joints well before their time.

On front-wheel-drive cars, look at the CV joints in the front axles. Are the boots intact? You may have been able to only check the inner CV joints while you were locking from the engine-compartment side, so now look at the outer joint boots. Once a boot is torn or cracked, moisture and dirt can get into the CV joint and ruin it. They are expensive to replace!

You examined the tires from the outside in your initial inspection, but now look at the backside of the tires. Check for repairs to the sidewalls, for cuts or abrasions, or serious weather-checking. Rear tires with excessive inner tread wear are hard to spot from the outside, unless you have the car raised as we do. Usually, inner tread wear on rear tires indicates that the tires got that way while on the front of the car, and have been switched to the rear to make way for new front tires or to disguise their wear pattern by being less visible in back.

You'll find a checklist at the end of this Chapter, which

Tip

Tire tread wear patterns can often be difficult to interpret, since there's usually more than one uneven-wear force at work. A professional who is also checking the suspension and steering systems is best able to make a judgement.

succinctly identifies all of the various visual inspections and operational checks we have outlined in the text. It can be hard to remember everything you're supposed to be looking for, especially if you are excited about finding the car you want. Photocopy our Haynes checklist and bring it with you (with a clipboard and pen) when you go to check out that next hot vehicle prospect.

Used Car Buying

Detailed Inspection Checklist

Underhood checks

Overall condition and cleanliness

Drivebelts
☐ Good ☐ Fair ☐ Poor

Vacuum lines and fittings
☐ Good ☐ Fair ☐ Poor

Electrical wiring
☐ Good ☐ Fair ☐ Poor

Battery
☐ Good ☐ Fair ☐ Poor

Battery box
☐ Good ☐ Fair ☐ Poor

Battery hold-downs
☐ Good ☐ Fair ☐ Poor

Distributor cap
☐ Good ☐ Fair ☐ Poor

Spark plug wires
☐ Good ☐ Fair ☐ Poor

Air filter
☐ Good ☐ Fair ☐ Poor

Electrical relay boxes
☐ Good ☐ Fair ☐ Poor

Windshield washer reservoir
☐ Good ☐ Fair ☐ Poor

PCV valve
☐ Good ☐ Fair ☐ Poor

Fluid level and quality checks:

Oil
☐ Good ☐ Fair ☐ Poor

Brake master cylinder fluid
☐ Good ☐ Fair ☐ Poor

Clutch master cylinder fluid
☐ Good ☐ Fair ☐ Poor

Power steering fluid
☐ Good ☐ Fair ☐ Poor

Transmission fluid
☐ Good ☐ Fair ☐ Poor

Coolant
☐ Good ☐ Fair ☐ Poor

Fluid leaks

General

Power steering
☐ Good ☐ Fair ☐ Poor

Oil
☐ Good ☐ Fair ☐ Poor

Transmission fluid
☐ Good ☐ Fair ☐ Poor

Brake fluid
☐ Good ☐ Fair ☐ Poor

Clutch master cylinder
☐ Good ☐ Fair ☐ Poor

Cooling system

Radiator
☐ Good   ☐ Fair   ☐ Poor

Radiator hoses
☐ Good   ☐ Fair   ☐ Poor

Heater hoses
☐ Good   ☐ Fair   ☐ Poor

Heater
☐ Good   ☐ Fair   ☐ Poor

Thermostat housing
☐ Good   ☐ Fair   ☐ Poor

Bypass hose
☐ Good   ☐ Fair   ☐ Poor

Coolant overflow tank
☐ Good   ☐ Fair   ☐ Poor

Air-conditioning

Hoses
☐ Good   ☐ Fair   ☐ Poor

Compressor
☐ Good   ☐ Fair   ☐ Poor

Condenser
☐ Good   ☐ Fair   ☐ Poor

Evaporator
☐ Good   ☐ Fair   ☐ Poor

Receiver-drier
☐ Good   ☐ Fair   ☐ Poor

Fuel

Fuel lines
☐ Good   ☐ Fair   ☐ Poor

Carburetor
☐ Good   ☐ Fair   ☐ Poor

Fuel injectors
☐ Good   ☐ Fair   ☐ Poor

Fuel filter
☐ Good   ☐ Fair   ☐ Poor

Fuel pump
☐ Good   ☐ Fair   ☐ Poor

Interior checks

Instrument operation
☐ Good   ☐ Fair   ☐ Poor

Air-conditioning operation
☐ Good   ☐ Fair   ☐ Poor

Blower switch operates at all speeds
☐ Good   ☐ Fair   ☐ Poor

Power antenna
☐ Good   ☐ Fair   ☐ Poor

Radio, tape or CD operation
☐ Good   ☐ Fair   ☐ Poor

Owner's manual
☐ Good   ☐ Fair   ☐ Poor

Maintenance records
☐ Good   ☐ Fair   ☐ Poor

Seat belts
☐ Good   ☐ Fair   ☐ Poor

Window operation, power or manual
☐ Good   ☐ Fair   ☐ Poor

Windshield wipers
☐ Good   ☐ Fair   ☐ Poor

Windshield washers
☐ Good   ☐ Fair   ☐ Poor

Cigarette lighter
☐ Good   ☐ Fair   ☐ Poor

(continued on next page)

Used Car Buying
Detailed Inspection Checklist (continued)

Interior checks (continued)

Clock
☐ Good ☐ Fair ☐ Poor

Map light, dome light
☐ Good ☐ Fair ☐ Poor

Alarm system
☐ Good ☐ Fair ☐ Poor

Door locks, power or manual
☐ Good ☐ Fair ☐ Poor

Remote operation of locks
☐ Good ☐ Fair ☐ Poor

Window tint film
☐ Good ☐ Fair ☐ Poor

Power mirrors
☐ Good ☐ Fair ☐ Poor

Rear window wiper
☐ Good ☐ Fair ☐ Poor

Rear window defroster
☐ Good ☐ Fair ☐ Poor

Convertible top operation
☐ Good ☐ Fair ☐ Poor

Condition of plastic rear window (convertible)
☐ Good ☐ Fair ☐ Poor

Sunroof or T-top
☐ Good ☐ Fair ☐ Poor

Seat adjustments
☐ Good ☐ Fair ☐ Poor

Power seat operation
☐ Good ☐ Fair ☐ Poor

Console
☐ Good ☐ Fair ☐ Poor

Glove box
☐ Good ☐ Fair ☐ Poor

Emergency brake
☐ Good ☐ Fair ☐ Poor

Maintenance/service stickers
☐ Good ☐ Fair ☐ Poor

Interior fuel-filler door release
☐ Good ☐ Fair ☐ Poor

Trunk Inspection

Proper key, key operation
☐ Good ☐ Fair ☐ Poor

Decklid/hatch fit
☐ Good ☐ Fair ☐ Poor

Weatherstripping
☐ Good ☐ Fair ☐ Poor

Interior trunk release
☐ Good ☐ Fair ☐ Poor

Gas-assisted trunk/hatch struts
☐ Good ☐ Fair ☐ Poor

Paint match
☐ Good ☐ Fair ☐ Poor

Floormats
☐ Good ☐ Fair ☐ Poor

Spare tire
☐ Good ☐ Fair ☐ Poor

Factory jack and tire-changing tools
☐ Good ☐ Fair ☐ Poor

Rust under floormat
☐ Good ☐ Fair ☐ Poor

Collision damage
☐ Good ☐ Fair ☐ Poor

Trailer wiring
☐ Good ☐ Fair ☐ Poor

Speaker wiring
☐ Good ☐ Fair ☐ Poor

Trunk courtesy light
☐ Good ☐ Fair ☐ Poor

TRUNK OPEN light on dash
☐ Good ☐ Fair ☐ Poor

Undercar Checks

CV joint boots
☐ Good ☐ Fair ☐ Poor

Exhaust system leaks
☐ Good ☐ Fair ☐ Poor

Exhaust system hangers
☐ Good ☐ Fair ☐ Poor

Non-stock exhaust components
☐ Good ☐ Fair ☐ Poor

Chassis (frame or unibody) condition
☐ Good ☐ Fair ☐ Poor

Driveshaft
☐ Good ☐ Fair ☐ Poor

Tires, from backside
☐ Good ☐ Fair ☐ Poor

Fluid leaks:

Fuel
☐ Good ☐ Fair ☐ Poor

Oil
☐ Good ☐ Fair ☐ Poor

Coolant
☐ Good ☐ Fair ☐ Poor

Power steering fluid
☐ Good ☐ Fair ☐ Poor

Transmission fluid
☐ Good ☐ Fair ☐ Poor

Rear transmission seal
☐ Good ☐ Fair ☐ Poor

Rear axle pinion seal
☐ Good ☐ Fair ☐ Poor

Brake lines:

Leaks
☐ Good ☐ Fair ☐ Poor

Crushed spots
☐ Good ☐ Fair ☐ Poor

Rust
☐ Good ☐ Fair ☐ Poor

Front suspension checks:

Shocks
☐ Good ☐ Fair ☐ Poor

Springs
☐ Good ☐ Fair ☐ Poor

Ball joints
☐ Good ☐ Fair ☐ Poor

Tie rod ends
☐ Good ☐ Fair ☐ Poor

Steering gear
☐ Good ☐ Fair ☐ Poor

Brakes
☐ Good ☐ Fair ☐ Poor

(continued on next page)

Used Car Buying
Detailed Inspection Checklist (continued)

Front suspension checks (continued):

Bushings

☐ Good   ☐ Fair   ☐ Poor

Rear Suspension checks:

Shocks

☐ Good   ☐ Fair   ☐ Poor

Springs

☐ Good   ☐ Fair   ☐ Poor

Brakes

☐ Good   ☐ Fair   ☐ Poor

Rear axle pinion seal

☐ Good   ☐ Fair   ☐ Poor

Bushings

☐ Good   ☐ Fair   ☐ Poor

Notes

_____
_____
_____
_____
_____
_____
_____
_____
_____
_____
_____
_____

5 The Professional Check

This is the final phase of our guide to thoroughly examining a used car or truck. After you have made your own initial inspection, taken a test-drive, and then made a more detailed examination yourself, there's nothing left to do except ask the advice of a professional mechanic.

Chances are, the vehicle should be a good buy if it has passed all the points of the stringent examination we have discussed so far in this book. However, it is possible there may be some nagging suspicions in one or two areas, and this is where the experienced hand/eye/ear of a mechanic can save you thousands of dollars in unwanted repairs. He has the background, training and specialized equipment to make more scientific, quantitative tests of most aspects of a car's condition.

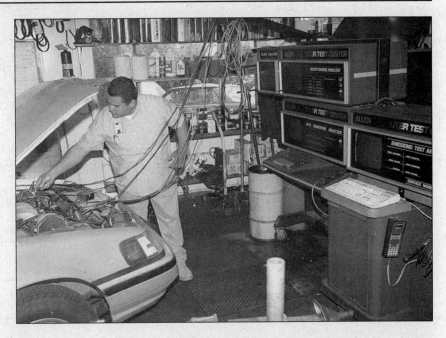

Not every mechanic will make every test we have outlined here, and on the other hand, your mechanic may want to perform some tests we have not suggested. Hiring a mechanic to perform the complete list of tests could be an expensive check-out for a used car! Many of the tests would be done by the mechanic only after making a preliminary evaluation, listening to the engine and making a thorough visual examination. He may even want to take his own short test-drive. What he suspects from the above evaluation will prompt him to perform the necessary tests to eliminate or confirm potential trouble areas.

Who should make the tests? If you already have a favorite shop or mechanic, take the car there. Trust is an important factor, since you are banking on this evaluation for a purchase that make take you years to pay off. If you don't have a trusted mechanic, trust referrals from friends and relatives who have had good success with a shop or individual in your area. Check the classified section in your local newspaper or the yellow pages in your telephone book. You may find ads for mobile mechanics, who work out of a van or truck performing tune-ups and light mechanical work at any location, even your own driveway. Some even specialize in used car inspections. They may not have every diagnostic tool on hand on their truck, but they may be able to actually meet you at a car lot or private-party location to examine a vehicle. This may be an important factor when purchasing from a private party who doesn't want to let you take the vehicle away for diagnostic testing.

In many large cities you will find independent diagnostic centers whose main business is inspection and diagnosis for a fee. You may be able to source out a trustworthy site through your local Better Business Bureau, Bureau of Automotive Repair, State Department of Consumer Affairs, or through the local auto club. The AAA (American Automobile Association) in your area may have a list of approved local diagnostic centers. Generally, their recommendations are consistently updated and trustworthy.

All this preparation and leg work may seem like a lot of trouble, but if you have ever had a friend or acquaintance who has experienced major problems after buying a used car, you'll realize the inconvenience is well worth it. Remember that the best protection against fraud, misleading appearances or hidden problems is a thorough pre-purchase examination such as we have suggested in this book. While we are on the subject of misleading appearances, don't assume self-righteously that if you discover a serious defect or problem with the vehicle you are inspecting, the seller is consciously trying to deceive you. Your thoroughness may have uncovered problems the seller probably wasn't aware of. In fact, if a private party or dealer seems reluctant to have you make a thorough examination and have the vehicle further tested by a mechanic, assure them that they may have a copy of any checklists or reports on the vehicle's condition. A printed report, prepared at your expense, might prove of benefit to the seller in remedying apparent problems and making their car more appealing. The cost of having a full diagnostic check made by a professional is relatively inexpensive compared to the potential costs of buying a defective vehicle. Because of the expense, we recommend you proceed with this last step in the inspection process only after you have made your own inspection and test-drive, and are fairly certain this is the right car at the right price for you going in.

Be aware that a mechanic who's looking for work may be motivated to encourage the purchase, even when the vehicle has problems. Remember that the actual purchase decision must be yours. The mechanic is simply providing technical information and a cost estimate to repair the vehicle, which is the information you need to ultimately negoti-

ate the purchase price of the vehicle.

For convenience, we suggest that you photocopy the checklist at the end of this chapter for your mechanic's reference. The glossary associated with this checklist explains briefly each of the mechanic's tests, and we have included a photo sequence of a professional mechanic performing many of the tests and inspections we have described. As stated earlier, it may not be necessary for your mechanic to perform all of these tests, you and your mechanic will decide which tests may be excluded.

Description of professional tests

Underhood checks

Check the fluids and fluid levels

Basically these are the same checks we have suggested the buyer make in Chapter 4, but the professional mechanic can make such checks quicker and with an experienced eye. He is looking for any fluid leaks and checking the "quality" of the fluids, looking at the color, smell and content of the car's fluids, anything that might hint to a possible problem area.

Check the belts, hoses and filters

Again, the checks are repetitive of your previous detailed inspection, but the professional mechanic may notice something you missed. An experienced mechanic is better qualified to inspect the sometimes confusing array of emission system hoses found on today's modern automobile. Often emissions system hoses are disconnected or missing and in many States must be brought back to factory specifications before the vehicle can be registered.

> **Tip**
>
> If you have reason to suspect the mileage shown on the odometer may not be accurate, ask the mechanic to also give his assessment - professionals know tell-tale signs to look for that can indicate fraudulent mileage readings.

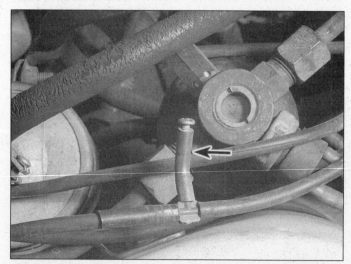

The mechanic will start with a visual inspection, much like you have made, except that experience has taught him just what to look for, like finding this plugged vacuum hose (arrow)

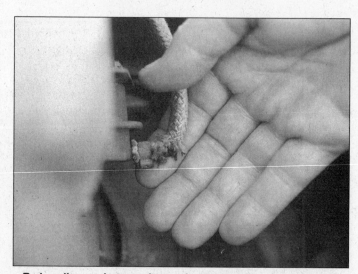

By bending and squeezing various vacuum, fuel, water and other hoses, the pro can turn up hidden problems like this splitting, cloth-covered European-style vacuum hose

While the average person might have missed this, our mechanic didn't - this disconnected heater hose was tucked under other components, to disguise the fact that the heater core had been blocked off and was probably defective

Only a sharp-eyed pro would spot that this accelerator/cruise control bracket (arrow) is missing its bottom leg and its mounting bolts

Listen for any unusual noises

Your mechanic is familiar with the sounds associated with good and bad engines. He can distinguish the difference between lifter noise and connecting-rod knock. He knows the difference between belt squeal from a worn-out, glazed drivebelt and an equivalent noise a defective power-steering pump, air conditioning compressor or alternator might make. He may be able to inform you, just from listening to the engine, of possible defects.

Check the timing belt

If the vehicle is approaching the 60,000-mile mark (this point varies with the make and model), it is probably due for a new timing belt. The mechanic can confirm this by remov-

A quick check of the air filter element and the cleanliness of the air filter housing can tell the mechanic something about the maintenance of the vehicle

A mechanic's stethoscope is used to pinpoint the exact location of a particular engine noise

If in doubt about the condition of a timing belt merely based on indicated mileage, a mechanic may remove the upper belt cover for a close inspection

A quick check with a timing light can confirm whether an engine is currently in tune

Even without a large, sophisticated analysis machine, a technician can use smaller instruments like this one to check volts, ohms, point dwell and engine speed

The mechanic uses an ohmmeter to check the actual resistance of each plug wire, which will tell him if any wire is out-of-specifications

Tip

On many vehicles a failed timing belt can lead to serious engine damage due to valve-to-piston interference. Any timing belt in marginal condition must be replaced!

ing one or more of the timing belt covers to inspect the belt for cracks and wear.

Engine diagnostic checks

Engine analyzer tests

By connecting a Diagnostic Engine Analyzer to the engine's electrical system, a mechanic can tell a great deal in a short time about the condition of the ignition system, charging system, timing and engine internal performance.

While the engine is running on an analyzer the mechanic can perform a **Power balance test** in which he selectively cancels each cylinder, one at a time. He watches the rpm drop when each cylinder is canceled, and if one cylinder has less rpm drop when canceled than the others, it means that cylinder is acting "weak", either from an ignition problem, which the scope could pinpoint, or from a mechanical problem (valves, rings, etc.), which would lead the mechanic to further tests to determine the cause.

The mechanic will also perform an **Ignition system primary and secondary circuit test.** By watching the patterns on the oscilloscope, the condition of coil, rotor, cap, spark plugs and spark plug wires can be checked. If any of these components are suspected of defects, they can be tested with smaller hand-held pieces of test equipment.

A state smog test isn't designed to give you a report on a used car, but a pro with the emissions-testing equipment can learn a lot about an engine's condition and state-of-tune

While in the shop's bay, a mechanic can quickly check the condition of the charging and starting systems

Test the exhaust emissions

The vehicle may also be connected to an exhaust-gas-analyzer by inserting a probe into the tailpipe. With the car running in Neutral, the mechanic can check the amount of carbon monoxide (CO) and hydrocarbons (HC) in the exhaust (other emissions can be tested with more sophisticated analyzers, but these two reveal a great deal). He will check the engine at idle and at higher rpm, comparing the results to specs for that specific make and model of vehicle. A good test means that the engine's carburetion/fuel injection is working efficiently. Engine mechanical problems such as worn rings, valves, and valve guides can also be detected through an emissions test.

Test the charging system and starter draw

In this test, a charging and starting system analyzer is connected to the alternator and battery. With the engine running, the output and regulation of the charging system is checked with the meters.

The condition of the starter is tested while the engine is cranked for 10 to 15 seconds. This test shows how many amps the starter is drawing, and is compared to specifications. Too much amperage draw could indicate a bad starter.

The battery condition is checked by performing a load test. A defective battery can further be diagnosed by sampling the electrolyte in the cells. The battery date code will also be checked.

Tip

In some states, an emissions check will be required before you can register the vehicle in your name. If not provided by the seller, it may be wise to get the required state certification at this time.

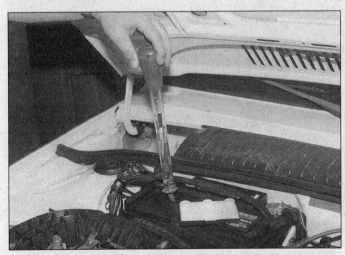

A battery hydrometer is used to check the state-of-charge of the battery

On computer-managed engines, a shop can hook up a code scanner that will read any maintenance or component fault codes that the computer is storing

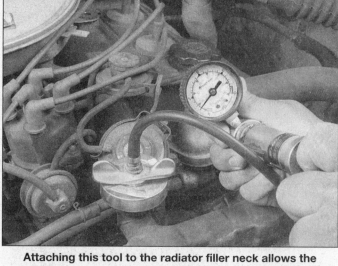

Attaching this tool to the radiator filler neck allows the mechanic to pressurize the cooling system, checking for possible leaks

> ## Tip
>
> On many vehicles, trouble codes can be displayed without any special tools – see the Haynes Computer Codes book for details.

Check the sensors and pull computer codes

On computer managed engines (most cars from 1980 on), problems with various components and systems are recorded in the computer in the form of codes. With a "scan" tool, a mechanic can recall any codes that indicate problem areas. New-car dealerships have the most sophisticated equipment for this test, but many independent shops also have scan tools now.

Pressure-check the cooling system

The cooling system is pressurized with a small hand-pump connected in place of the vehicle's radiator cap. The radiator, hoses, gaskets and any other potential areas of leakage are then inspected. Any leaks or problem areas in the cooling system will immediately be located by the presence of antifreeze.

Test the coolant/antifreeze

Sampling the coolant from the radiator with a hydrometer will reveal the amount of freezing/corrosion protection (ratio of antifreeze to water) in the coolant.

Check the air conditioning system

You may have noted in your detailed inspection that the air conditioning system was inoperative. Your mechanic can check the system with a set of gauges to determine the extent of repairs. If a low refrigerant charge is found, have him perform a refrigerant leak check to determine the point of escaping refrigerant.

The amount and condition of antifreeze can easily and quickly be checked with a coolant hydrometer

By connecting a set of air conditioning system test gauges your mechanic will be able to evaluate the performance of the air conditioning system

An electronic leak-detector can quickly test an air conditioning system for the presence of escaping refrigerant

Check the cylinder compression

If the cylinder balance test indicated there might be an internal mechanical problem, the spark plugs are removed and a pressure gauge is inserted into each spark plug hole, one cylinder at a time. When the engine is cranked for a few seconds, the gauge registers the compression developed, and can precisely indicate weak cylinders in terms of leaky valves, worn rings or a blown head gasket.

Test for combustion gas in the coolant

Not every shop has this particular test device (although almost all radiator shops do), but if the balance test and compression test indicated a problem, this test might be called for. A device samples coolant from the radiator with the engine running at high idle, and a test liquid changes color if there are combustion gasses present. If so, it indicates either a crack in the block or head(s), or a blown head gasket.

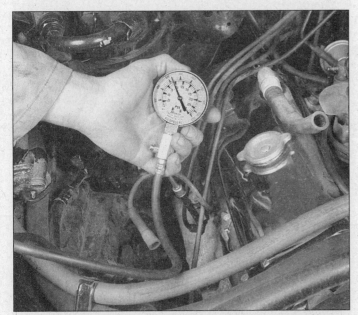

A cylinder compression check is performed with a gauge threaded into the spark plug hole - your mechanic will test all the cylinders, looking for one or more with low compression, indicating major mechanical problems

A tester like this takes a sample from the radiator, and if there are any combustion gasses present (signs of an engine internal problem), the test fluid changes from blue to yellow

The Haynes Used Car Buying Guide

Besides the expensive test equipment he can utilize, the second reason for letting a mechanic check out your car prospect is that he has access to a hoist, where inspection of the underside can be much more thorough

Here the mechanic is pointing out an aftermarket suspension modification that has been made to this Sable - this modification makes rear wheel-alignment much easier and is a "plus point" for the vehicle

Check for TSB's

If the vehicle is being checked out at a new-car dealership of the same make, The service department will run the original warranty card through their computer to check the car's record for recall notices. They can determine if these recall "fixes" have actually been performed. They can also check their records for Technical Service Bulletins, which the manufacturers issue regularly to update mechanics on potential problem areas to look at on specific models. Some independent shops have access to these TSB's on their computer. They could, for instance, tell you that the transmission for that model had a lot of recalls or TSB's, and it may not be a good used-car buy in terms of reliability.

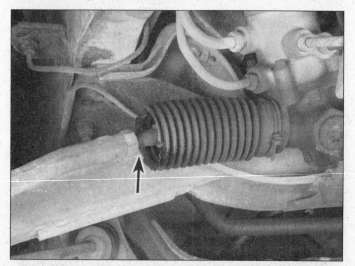

The torn boot (arrow) on this rack-and-pinion steering gear wasn't visible from looking under the front end, but was immediately noticed by a mechanic with a lift

> **Tip**
> Federal law requires auto manufacturers to make TSB's public, although dealerships often try to avoid giving them out for obvious reasons. Don't let them intimidate you. The registered owner of a vehicle has the right to demand to see all relevant TSB's.

Undercar checks

Having access to a hoist is one of the key reasons you are bringing the vehicle to a professional for an inspection. A great deal can be examined when inspecting from underneath. The mechanic will thoroughly go over most of the points we suggested in Chapter 4, but again, his experienced eye can check better and faster than an amateur.

Check the suspension and steering systems

Besides the visual examination, he will check the suspension and steering components front and rear, looking for wear, collision damage and evidence of proper lubrication and maintenance. A mechanic equipped with a hoist can check the balljoints for wear, which can be unsafe if worn excessively. Ask your mechanic for his opinion of the

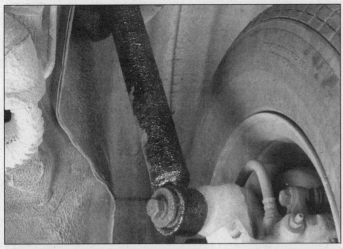

This oil-soaked shock absorber represents a repair of several hundred dollars (for all four shocks), a major bargaining chip for you

With a lift, these balljoint boots can be easily checked for damage

With the vehicle raised up, the mechanic can put a block under one front wheel and lower the chassis to where there is only half a load on the spring, and then check the wear/movement of the balljoints with a prybar

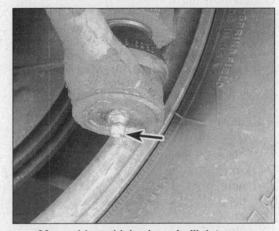

Many older vehicles have balljoint wear indicators - a close inspection reveals whether the grease fittings (arrow) have receded, indicated wear

By moving the tire/wheel in and out at the bottom, the condition of the wheel bearings and other suspension elements can be determined

Your mechanic is well-equipped to inspect tires and diagnose what may have caused a particular pattern of uneven wear

The Haynes Used Car Buying Guide

The experienced pro can remove all four of the vehicle's wheels for a thorough inspection of calipers, hoses and other brake components

Flexible brake hoses should always be given close scrutiny - this cracked hose must be replaced

tires. If there's any abnormal tread wear present, he'll give you his evaluation.

Check the braking system

Have your mechanic remove all four wheels, allowing him to carefully inspect the front and rear brakes, pad/shoe thickness, rotor thickness, wheel cylinder/caliper condition and emergency-brake linkages. In minutes, he can tell you approximately how much life is left in the current brake materials before needing a brake job.

Check the driveline/driveaxles

Your mechanic should inspect the driveshaft and rear axle on rear-wheel drive vehicles. He'll be looking for defective U-joints and rear axle seal leaks. On front-wheel drive

vehicles the driveaxle boots and constant-velocity joints will be inspected.

Check for fluid leaks

With the vehicle raised on a hoist its any easy matter to thoroughly inspect the undercarriage for any leaking components. Automobiles are notorious for leaking oil and fluids. Your mechanic will advise you on the seriousness of any leaks found. Minor leaks may be acceptable on a used car while major oil leaks and *any* fuel leaks should be repaired immediately.

Check the exhaust system

An exhaust system check will be performed, paying special attention to the catalytic converter and muffler. Also

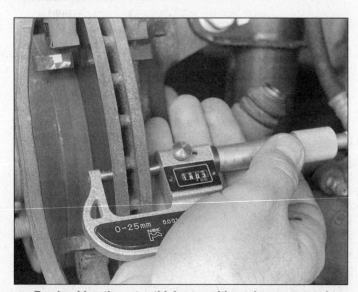

By checking the rotor thickness with a micrometer and comparing this to specifications, an approximation of the useful life left in the rotors can be made

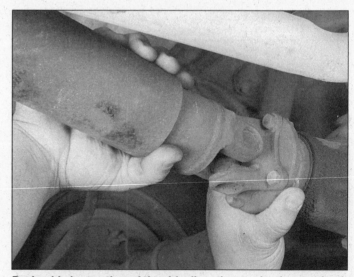

During his inspection of the driveline, the mechanic can check the U-joints by twisting each side in opposite directions to check for play - he'll also check the pinion-shaft play and pinion seal

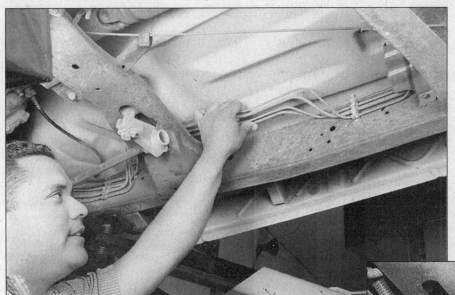

While on the hoist, it only takes a minute to check the full length of hoses and lines along the chassis

Tip

Exhaust system components are usually the first components on a car to rust through. Since exhaust gas is poisonous, you should always immediately replace any exhaust system components that are rusted through.

The wet spot on this fuel filler hose (arrow) indicated a potentially dangerous gasoline leak

Weeping transmission fluid here (arrow) implies that the transmission rear seal needs replacing

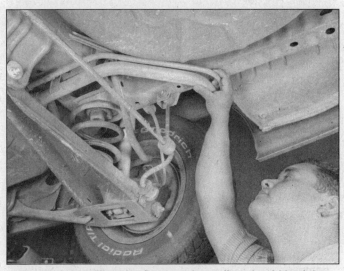

The fuel tank filler pipe/hose and vent line should both be checked for damage or restrictions

Check the exhaust system (continued)

Besides pointing out defects like these exhaust system holes, the pro can tell you the priorities - which items need immediate attention and the relative costs of fixing various components and systems

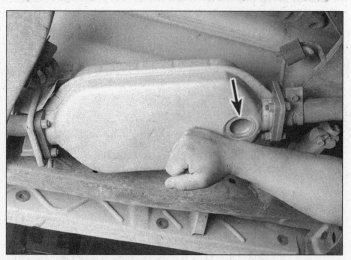

The emissions test will tell if the catalytic converter is working properly, and on older GM-type converters, the mechanic may hit the converter to see if the pellets rattle (they should) - only those converters that have a drain plug (arrow) have pellets

ask your mechanic to note any exhaust leaks. Some vehicles are notorious for cracking exhaust manifolds, which can be an expensive repair.

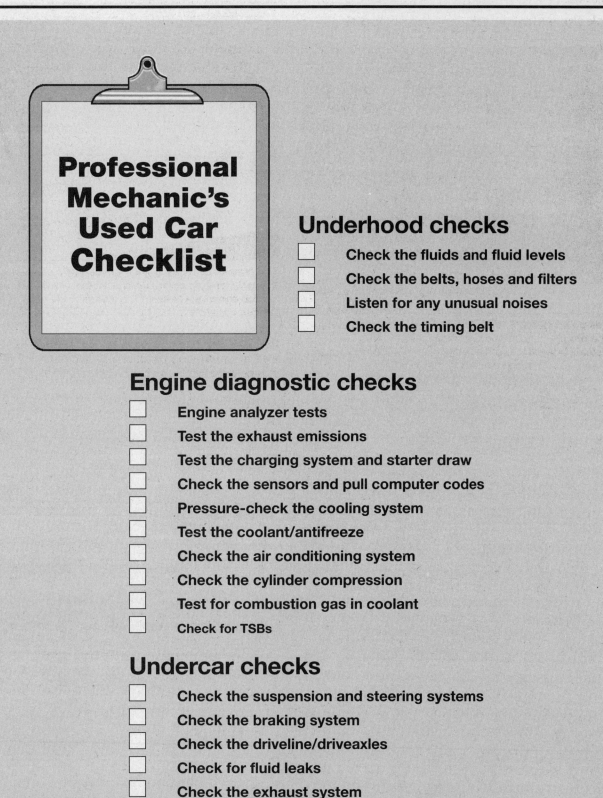

Professional Mechanic's Used Car Checklist

Underhood checks

- [ ] Check the fluids and fluid levels
- [ ] Check the belts, hoses and filters
- [ ] Listen for any unusual noises
- [ ] Check the timing belt

Engine diagnostic checks

- [ ] Engine analyzer tests
- [ ] Test the exhaust emissions
- [ ] Test the charging system and starter draw
- [ ] Check the sensors and pull computer codes
- [ ] Pressure-check the cooling system
- [ ] Test the coolant/antifreeze
- [ ] Check the air conditioning system
- [ ] Check the cylinder compression
- [ ] Test for combustion gas in coolant
- [ ] Check for TSBs

Undercar checks

- [ ] Check the suspension and steering systems
- [ ] Check the braking system
- [ ] Check the driveline/driveaxles
- [ ] Check for fluid leaks
- [ ] Check the exhaust system

Notes

The Haynes Used Car Buying Guide

Appendix A
Vehicle Identification Number (VIN) guide

The Vehicle Identification Number, or VIN number, as it's usually called, is a long string of numbers and letters imprinted on a small plate located on the driver's side of the dashboard. Everybody knows that these numbers are the means by which a vehicle is identified by the state in which the vehicle is licensed and registered. But what most people *don't* know is that those numbers mean a lot more than simply the "number" of a vehicle. Once you know what each individual number or letter represents, you can learn all sorts of information about your vehicle. We'll only deal with the two most important characters of the VIN - the model year code and the engine code (which will reveal the number of cylinders, displacement and in some cases, the type of fuel system). Always refer to the VIN number when you're buying parts for your vehicle.

AMERICAN MOTORS CORP.

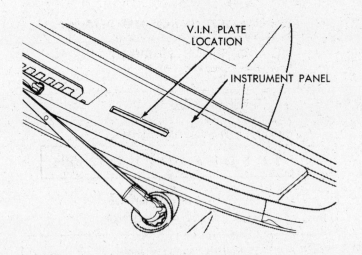

V.I.N. PLATE
LOCATION

INSTRUMENT PANEL

Example (1974 through 1980 models):

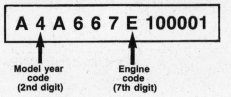

A 4 A 6 6 7 E 100001

Model year
code
(2nd digit)

Engine
code
(7th digit)

Example (1981 through 1988 models):

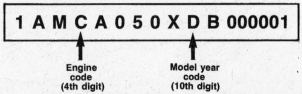

1 A M C A 0 5 0 X D B 000001

Engine
code
(4th digit)

Model year
code
(10th digit)

Engine codes

1974

A	6	258
E	6	232
H	8	304
N	8	360 (2 barrel)
P	8	360 (4 barrel)
Z	8	401

1975

A	6	258
E	6	232
H	8	304
N	8	360 (2 barrel)
P	8	360 (4 barrel)
Z	8	401

1976

A	6	258 (1 barrel)
C	6	258 (2 barrel)
E	6	232
H	8	304
N	8	360 (2 barrel)
P	8	360 (4 barrel)
Z	8	401

1977

A	6	258 (1 barrel)
C	6	258 (2 barrel)
E	6	232
H	8	304

N	8	360
S	4	121

1978

A	6	258 (1 barrel)
C	6	258 (2 barrel)
E	6	232
G	4	121
H	8	304
N	8	360

1979

A	6	258 (1 barrel)
C	6	258 (2 barrel)
E	6	232
G	4	121
H	8	304

1980

B	4	151
C	6	258

1981 - 1983

B	4	151
C	6	258
U	4	151

1984

C	6	258
U	4	151
V	4	151 (export)

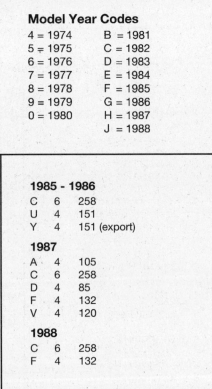

Model Year Codes

4 = 1974	B = 1981
5 = 1975	C = 1982
6 = 1976	D = 1983
7 = 1977	E = 1984
8 = 1978	F = 1985
9 = 1979	G = 1986
0 = 1980	H = 1987
	J = 1988

1985 - 1986

C	6	258
U	4	151
Y	4	151 (export)

1987

A	4	105
C	6	258
D	4	85
F	4	132
V	4	120

1988

C	6	258
F	4	132

CHRYSLER CORP.

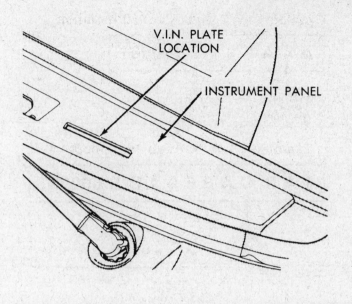

V.I.N. PLATE LOCATION

INSTRUMENT PANEL

Example (1974 through 1980 models):

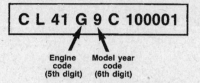

C L 41 G 9 C 100001

Engine code (5th digit)
Model year code (6th digit)

Example (1981 and later models):

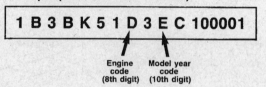

1 B 3 B K 5 1 D 3 E C 100001

Engine code (8th digit)
Model year code (10th digit)

Model Year Codes

4 = 1974	B = 1981	J = 1988
5 = 1975	C = 1982	K = 1989
6 = 1976	D = 1983	L = 1990
7 = 1977	E = 1984	M = 1991
8 = 1978	F = 1985	N = 1992
9 = 1979	G = 1986	P = 1993
0 = 1980	H = 1987	R = 1994

Engine codes

1974

B	6	198
C	6	225
E	6	(special order)
G	8	318
J	8	360 (200 H.P.)
K	8	360 (180 H.P.)
L	8	360 (245 H.P.)
M	8	400 (185 H.P.)
N	8	400 (205 H.P.)
P	8	400 (250 H.P.)
T	8	440 (230 H.P.)
U	8	440 (250 H.P.)
Z	8	(special order)

1975

C	6	225
E	6	(special order)
G	8	318
J	8	360 (190 H.P.)
K	8	360 (180 H.P.)
L	8	360 (230 H.P.)
M	8	400 (165 H.P.)
N	8	400 (195 H.P.)
P	8	400 (235 H.P.)
T	8	440 (215 H.P.)
U	8	440 (260 H.P.)
Z	8	(special order)

1976

C	6	225
E	6	(special order)
G	8	318
J	8	360 (175 H.P.)
K	8	360 (170 H.P.)
L	8	360 (220 H.P.)
M	8	400 (175 H.P.)
N	8	400 (185 H.P.)

P	8	400 (240 H.P.)
T	8	440 (205 H.P.)
U	8	440 (250 H.P.)
Z	8	(special order)

1977

C	6	225 (100 H.P.)
D	6	225 (110 H.P.)
E	6	(special order)
G	8	318
J	8	360 (170 H.P.)
K	8	360 (155 H.P.)
L	8	360 (175 H.P.)
N	8	400 (190 H.P.)
P	8	400 (190 H.P.)
T	8	440 (195 H.P.)
U	8	440 (240 H.P.)
Z	8	(special order)

1978

A	4	105
C	6	225 (100 H.P.)
D	6	225 (110 H.P.)
E	6	(special order)
G	8	318 (140 H.P.)
H	8	318 (155 H.P.)
J	8	360 (170 H.P.)
K	8	360 (155 H.P.)
L	8	360 (175 H.P.)
N	8	400 (190 H.P.)
P	8	400 (190 H.P., heavy duty)
T	8	440 (195 H.P.)
U	8	440 (240 H.P.)
Z	8	(special order)

1979

A	4	105
C	6	225 (100 H.P.)

D	6	225 (110 H.P.)
E	6	(special order)
G	8	318 (135 H.P.)
H	8	318 (155 H.P.)
J	8	360 (170 H.P.)
K	8	360 (150 H.P.)
L	8	360 (195 H.P.)
Z	8	(special order)

1980

A	4	105
C	6	225 (90 H.P.)
E	6	(special order)
G	8	318 (120 H.P.)
H	8	318 (155 H.P.)
K	8	360 (130 H.P.)
L	8	360 (185 H.P.)
Z	8	(special order)

1981

A	4	105
B	4	135
D	4	156
E	6	225 (1 barrel)
F	6	225 (1 barrel heavy duty)
G	6	225 (2 barrel)
H	6	225 (2 barrel heavy duty)
J	8	318 (fuel injection)
K	8	318 (2 barrel)
L	8	318 (2 barrel heavy duty)
M	8	318 (4 barrel)
N	8	318 (4 barrel heavy duty)

1982

A	4	105
B	4	135
C	4	135 (turbocharged)

Chrysler (continued)

D	4	156
E	6	225 (1 barrel)
F	6	225 (1 barrel heavy duty)
G	6	225 (2 barrel)
H	6	225 (2 barrel heavy duty)
J	8	318 (fuel injection)
K	8	318 (2 barrel)
L	8	318 (2 barrel heavy duty)
M	8	318 (4 barrel)
N	8	318 (4 barrel heavy duty)

1983

A	4	97
B	4	105
C	4	135
E	4	135 (turbocharged)
F	4	135 (high performance)
G	4	156
H	6	225 (1 barrel)
J	6	225 (1 barrel heavy duty)
K	6	225 (2 barrel)

1984

A	4	97
C	4	135
D	4	135 (fuel injection)
E	4	135 (turbocharged)
F	4	135 (high performance)
G	4	156
P	8	318 (2 barrel)
R	8	318 (4 barrel)
S	8	318 (police)
4	8	318 (heavy duty)
8	4	135 (high output)

1985 - 1986

A	4	97
C	4	135
D	4	135
E	4	135 (turbocharged)
F	4	135 (high performance)
G	4	156

K	4	153
P	8	318 (2 barrel)
R	8	318 (4 barrel)
S	8	318 (police)
4	8	318 (heavy duty)
8	4	135 (high output)

1987 - 1988

A	4	135 (intercooled, turbocharged)
C	4	135
D	4	135 (fuel injection)
E	4	135 (turbocharged)
F	4	98 (fuel injection, turbocharged)
F	4	122 (fuel injection, turbocharged)
G	4	156
H	4	156 (turbocharged)
K	4	153 (fuel injection)
N	4	156 (turbocharged)
P	8	318 (2 barrel)
R	8	318 (4 barrel)
S	8	318 (police)
X	4	135
Z	8	318
3	6	181 (fuel injection)
4	8	318 (heavy duty)
7	8	318
8	4	135 (high output)

1989 - 1990

A	4	135 (turbocharged)
C	4	135 (fuel injection, turbocharged)
D	4	135 (fuel injection)
H	4	150
J	4	153 (turbocharged)
K	4	153 (fuel injection)
N	4	156 (turbocharged)
P	8	318
R	4	135 (turbocharged)
S	8	318

T	4	107 (fuel injection)
U	6	180 (fuel injection)
V	4	122 (fuel injection)
X	4	90 (fuel injection)
Z	4	98 (fuel injection, turbocharged)
3	6	181 (fuel injection)
4	8	318

1991 -1992

3	6	181 (MFI)
A	4	90 (MFI)
A	4	135 (MFI turbo)
B	6	181 (MFI-24V)
B	6	201 (MFI)
C	6	181 (MFI turbo)
D	4	135 (EFI)
J	4	153 (MFI turbo)
K	4	153 (EFI)
L	6	231 (MFI)
R	6	201 (MFI)
S	6	181 (MFI)
U	6	180 (MFI)
V	4	122 (MFI)

1993 - 1994

A	4	90 (MPI)
C	4	112 (MPI)
G	4	144 (MPI)
B	4	112 (MPI)
E	4	122 (MPI)
F	4	122 (MPI turbo)
H	6	181 (MPI)
K	6	181 (MPI turbo)
D	4	133 (EFI)
A	4	133 (EFI turbo)
K	4	151 (EFI)
V	4	151 (MPI)
3	6	181 (MPI)
R	6	201 (MPI)
L	6	231 (MPI)
T	6	201 (SMPI)
F	6	216 (SMPI)

FORD MOTOR CO.

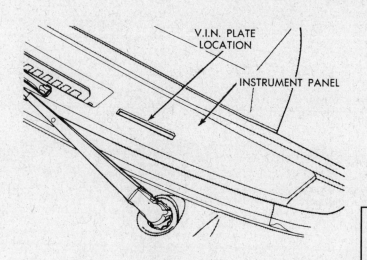

V.I.N. PLATE LOCATION

INSTRUMENT PANEL

Example (1974 through 1980 models):

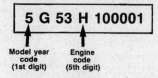

5 G 53 H 100001

Model year code (1st digit)

Engine code (5th digit)

Example (1981 and later models):

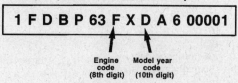

1 F D B P 63 F X D A 6 00001

Engine code (8th digit)

Model year code (10th digit)

Model Year Codes

4 = 1974	B = 1981	J = 1988
5 = 1975	C = 1982	K = 1989
6 = 1976	D = 1983	L = 1990
7 = 1977	E = 1984	M = 1991
8 = 1978	F = 1985	N = 1992
9 = 1979	G = 1986	P = 1993
0 = 1980	H = 1987	R = 1994

Engine codes

1974

A	8	460
C	8	460 (police)
F	8	302
H	8	351
L	6	250
Q	8	351 (Cobra Jet)
S	8	400
T	6	200
X	4	122
Y	4	140
Z	6	171

1975 - 1978

A	8	460
C	8	460 (police)
F	8	302
H	8	351
L	6	250
S	8	400
T	6	200
Y	4	140
Z	6	171

1979

F	8	302
H	8	351
L	6	250
S	8	400
T	6	200
W	4	140
Y	4	140
Z	6	171

1980

A	4	140
B	6	200
C	6	250
D	8	255
F	8	302
G	8	351
O		(special order)

1981

A	4	140
B	6	200
D	8	255
F	8	302
G	8	351
T	4	140
2	4	98

1982

A	4	140
B	6	200
D	8	255
F	8	302
G	8	351
2	4	98
3	6	232
6	4	140 (LP gas)

1983

A	4	140 (2 barrel)
D	4	140 (turbo)
F	8	302
G	8	351 (police)
R	4	140 (1 barrel)
W	4	140 (turbo)
X	6	200
2	4	98
3	6	232
4	4	98
5	4	98 (fuel injection)
6	4	140 (LP gas)

1984

A	4	140 (2 barrel)
F	8	302
G	8	351
H	4	122 (diesel)
L	6	146 (diesel)
M	8	302 (fuel injection)
R	4	140 (1 barrel)
W	4	140 (turbo)

2	4	98
3	6	232
4	4	98 (high output)
5	4	98 (fuel injection)
6	4	140 (LP gas)
7	4	98 (methanol)
8	4	98 (turbo)

1985 - 1986

A	4	140
C	6	232
D	4	153
F	8	302
G	8	351
H	4	122 (diesel)
J	4	113
L	6	146 (diesel)
M	8	302 (fuel injection)
R	4	140
S	4	140 (fuel injection)
T	4	140 (turbo)
U	6	183
W	4	140 (turbo)
X	4	140 (fuel injection)
2	4	98
3	6	232 (fuel injection)
4	4	98
5	4	98 (fuel injection)
6	4	140 (LP gas)
7	4	98 (methanol)
8	4	98 (turbo)
9	4	116

1987

A	4	140 (MFI)
D	4	153 (TBI)
E	8	302 (high output, 225 HP)
F	8	302 (MFI)
G	8	351 (2 barrel)

Ford (continued)

H	4	122 (diesel)
J	4	116 (MFI, high output)
M	8	302 (MFI, 200 HP, high output)
S	4	140 (TBI)
U	6	183 (MFI)
W	4	140 (MFI, turbocharged)
X	4	140 (TBI)
3	6	232 (TBI)
9	4	113 (TBI)

1988

A	4	140 (EFI)
D	4	153 (EFI)
E	8	302 (EFI, high output)
F	8	302 (EFI),
G	8	351 (police)
J	4	113 (EFI, high output)
K	4	79.3
S	4	140 (EFI)
U	6	183 (EFI)
W	4	140 (turbocharged EFI)
X	4	140 (EFI)
Y	4	140
3	6	232 (EFI)
4	6	232 (MFI)
5	4	98 (EFI)
9	4	113 (EFI)

1989 - 1990

A	4	140 (fuel injection)
C	4	133 (fuel injection)

C	6	232 (supercharged)
D	4	153 (fuel injection)
E	8	302 (fuel injection)
F	8	302 (fuel injection)
J	4	113 (fuel injection)
K	4	81
L	4	133 (fuel injection, turbocharged)
R	6	232 (supercharged)
S	4	140 (fuel injection)
U	6	182 (fuel injection)
X	4	140 (fuel injection)
Y	6	182 (fuel injection, DOHC)
4	6	232 (fuel injection)
5	4	98 (fuel injection)
9	4	116 (fuel injection)

1991 - 1992

4	6	232 (SFI)
6	4	98 (EFI turbo)
8	4	109 (EFI 16-V)
C	4	133 (EFI)
E	8	301 (SFI)
F	8	302 (SFI)
G	8	351 (carb 2.v)
H	4	81 (EFI)
J	4	114 (SFI)
L	4	133 (EFI turbo)
M	4	140 (EFI)
N	4	153 (SFI)
R	6	232 (SFI supercharged)
T	8	302 (SFI)

U	6	182 (SFI)
W	8	281 (SFI)
X	4	141 (SFI)
Y	6	182 (SFI)
Z	4	98 (EFI)

1993 - 1994

4	6	232 (SEFI)
6	4	98 (EFI)
8	4	109 (EFI)
A	4	122 (EFI)
B	6	153 (SEFI)
E	8	302 (SEFI)
H	4	81 (EFI)
J	4	114 (EFI)
M	4	141 (SEFI)
P	6	195 (SEFI)
R	6	232 (SEFI)
T	8	302 (SEFI)
U	6	182 (EFI)
V	8	281 (SEFI)
W	8	281 (SEFI)
X	4	141 (EFI)
Y	6	182 (SEFI)
Z	4	98 (EFI)

GENERAL MOTORS
Buick division

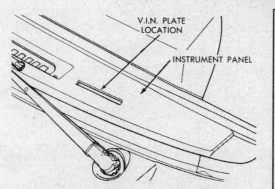

V.I.N. PLATE LOCATION

INSTRUMENT PANEL

Model Year Codes	
4 = 1974	B = 1981
5 = 1975	C = 1982
6 = 1976	D = 1983
7 = 1977	E = 1984
8 = 1978	F = 1985
9 = 1979	G = 1986
0 = 1980	H = 1987
	J = 1988
	K = 1989
	L = 1990
	M = 1991
	N = 1992
	P = 1993
	R = 1994

Example (1974 through 1980 models):

4 N 69 D 4 H 100001

Engine code (5th digit) Model year code (6th digit)

Example (1981 and later models):

1 G 1 A Z 37 A X D D 100001

Engine code (8th digit) Model year code (10th digit)

Engine codes

1974
D	6	250
H	8	350 (150 H.P.)
J	8	350 (175 H.P.)
P	8	455 (175 H.P.)
R	8	455 (190 H.P.)
T	8	455 (210 H.P.)
U	8	455 (230 H.P.)
V	8	455 (255 H.P.)
W	8	455 (245 H.P.)

1975
C	6	231
D	6	250
F	8	260
H	8	350 (145 H.P.)
J	8	350 (165 H.P.)
T	8	455

1976
C	6	231
F	8	260
H	8	350 (140 H.P.)
J	8	350 (155 H.P.)
T	8	455

1977
A	6	231 (even firing)
C	6	231 (uneven firing)
H	8	350 (140 H.P.)
J	8	350 (155 H.P.)
K	8	403
L	8	350 (170 H.P.)
R	8	350 (170 H.P.)
U	8	305
Y	8	301

1978
A	6	231 (105 H.P.)
C	6	196
G	6	231 (150 H.P.)
H	8	305 (100 H.P.)
K	8	403
L	8	350 (170 H.P.)
R	8	350 (170 H.P.)
U	8	305 (145 H.P.)
X	8	350 (155 H.P.)
Y	8	301
2	6	231
3	6	231 (165 H.P.)

1979
A	6	231 (2 barrel)
C	6	196
G	8	305 (2 barrel)
H	8	305 (4 barrel)
K	8	403
L	8	350
R	8	350
W	8	301 (4 barrel)
X	8	350
Y	8	301 (2 barrel)
2	6	231 (2 barrel)
3	6	231 (4 barrel)

1980
A	6	231 (2 barrel)
H	8	305
N	8	350 (diesel)
R	8	350
S	8	265
W	8	301
Y	8	307
X	8	350
3	6	231 (turbocharged)
4	6	252
5	4	151
7	6	173

1981
A	6	231
N	8	350 (diesel)
S	8	260
X	6	173
Y	8	307
3	6	231 (turbocharged)
4	6	252
5	4	151

1982
A	6	231
B	4	121
E	6	181
G	4	112 (2 barrel)
N	8	350 (diesel)
R	4	151
T	6	260 (diesel)
V	6	260 (diesel)
X	6	173
Y	8	307
Z	6	173
0	4	112 (fuel injected)
3	6	231 (turbocharged)
4	6	252

1983
A	6	231 (2 barrel)
B	4	121 (export)
E	6	181
H	8	307 (export)
N	8	350 (diesel)
P	4	121 (fuel injected)
R	4	151 (fuel injected)
T	6	260 (diesel)
V	6	260 (diesel)
X	6	173
Y	6	307
Z	6	173
0	4	112
4	6	252
5	4	151 (export)
8	6	231 (4 barrel)

1984
A	6	231 (2 barrel)
B	4	121 (export)
E	6	181
H	8	307
J	4	112 (fuel injected)
N	8	350 (diesel)
P	4	121 (fuel injected)
R	4	151 (fuel injected)
T	6	260 (diesel)
V	6	260 (diesel)
X	6	173
Y	8	307
Z	6	173
0	4	112 (fuel injected)
3	6	231 (fuel injected)
4	6	252
9	6	231 (fuel injected)

1985 - 1986
A	6	231
B	6	231 (fuel injected)
E	6	181
H	8	307
J	4	112 (fuel injected)
L	6	181 (fuel injected)
N	8	350 (diesel)
P	4	121 (fuel injected)
R	4	151 (fuel injected)
T	6	260 (diesel)
U	4	151 (fuel injected)
W	6	173 (fuel injected)
X	6	173
Y	8	307
0	4	112 (fuel injected)

1987 - 1988 (continued)
3	6	231 (fuel injected)
7	6	231 (turbo)
9	6	231 (fuel injected)

1987 - 1988
1	4	121 (TBI)
3	6	231 (SFI)
7	6	231 (turbocharged, SFI)
A	6	231 (2 barrel)
C	6	231 (fuel injection)
D	4	140 (fuel injection)
K	4	121 (OHC, TBI)
L	6	181 (MFI)
M	4	121 (turbocharged MFI)
R	4	151 (TBI)
U	4	151 (TBI)
W	6	173 (MFI)
Y	8	307 (4 barrel)

1989 - 1990
C	6	231 (fuel injection)
D	4	140 (fuel injection)
N	6	189 (fuel injection)
R	4	151 (fuel injection)
U	4	151 (fuel injection)
W	6	173 (fuel injection)
Y	8	307
1	4	121 (fuel injection)

1991 - 1992
1	6	231 (SFI supercharged)
7	8	350 (EFI)
D	4	138 (MFI)
E	8	305 (EFI)
L	6	231 (SFI)
N	6	204 (MFI)
R	4	151 (EFI)
T	6	191 (MFI)
U	4	151 (EFI)

1993 - 1994
1	6	231 (SFI supercharged)
3	4	138 (MFI)
4	4	133 (MFI)
7	8	350 (TBI)
L	6	231 (SFI)
M	6	191 (SFI)
N	6	204 (MFI)
P	8	350 (SFI)
T	6	191 (MFI)

GENERAL MOTORS
Cadillac division

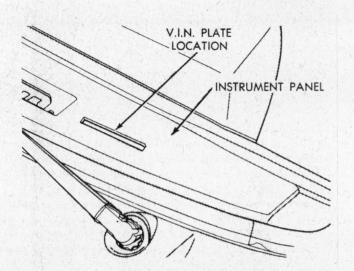

V.I.N. PLATE
LOCATION

INSTRUMENT PANEL

Example (1974 through 1980 models):

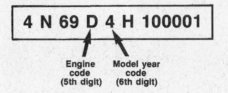

4 N 69 D 4 H 100001

Engine code (5th digit) → Model year code (6th digit)

Example (1981 and later models):

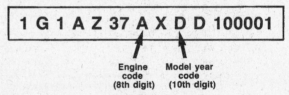

1 G 1 A Z 37 A X D D 100001

Engine code (8th digit) → Model year code (10th digit)

Model Year Codes

4 = 1974	B = 1981
5 = 1975	C = 1982
6 = 1976	D = 1983
7 = 1977	E = 1984
8 = 1978	F = 1985
9 = 1979	G = 1986
0 = 1980	H = 1987
	J = 1988
	K = 1989
	L = 1990
	M = 1991
	N = 1992
	P = 1993
	R = 1994

Engine codes

1974
R	8	472
S	8	500

1975
S	8	500
S	8	500 (fuel injection)

1976
R	8	350
S	8	500
S	8	500 (fuel injection)

1977
R	8	350
S	8	425
T	8	425 (fuel injection)

1978 - 1979
B	8	350 (fuel injection)
N	8	350 (diesel)
S	8	425
T	8	425 (fuel injection)

1980
4	6	252
6	8	368
8	8	350 (fuel injection)
9	8	368 (fuel injection)
N	8	350 (diesel)

1981
G	4	112
N	8	350 (diesel)
4	6	252
6	8	368
9	8	368 (fuel injection)

1982
B	4	121
G	4	112
N	8	350 (diesel)
4	6	252
8	8	252 (fuel injection)
9	8	368

1983
B	4	121 (export)
N	8	350 (diesel)
P	4	121 (fuel injection)
6	8	368
8	8	252
9	8	368

1984
B	4	121 (export)
N	8	350 (diesel)
P	4	121 (fuel injection)
8	8	252
9	8	368

1985 - 1986
N	8	350 (diesel)
P	4	121
T	6	260 (diesel)
W	6	173
Y	8	307
8	8	252

1987 - 1988
W	6	173 (MFI)
Y	8	307 (4 barrel)
5	8	273 (fuel injection)
7	8	250 (TBI)
8	8	250 (TBI)

1989 - 1990
Y	8	307
5	8	273 (fuel injection)
8	8	273 (fuel injection)

1991 - 1992
8	8	273 (SFI)
B	8	300 (SFI)

1993 - 1994
7	8	350 (TBI)
9	8	279 (TPI)
B	8	300 (SFI)
P	8	350 (SFI)

GENERAL MOTORS
Chevrolet division

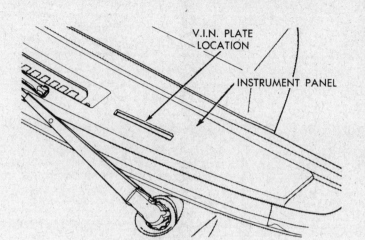

V.I.N. PLATE LOCATION

INSTRUMENT PANEL

Example (1974 through 1980 models):

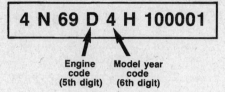

| 4 | N | 69 | D | 4 | H | 100001 |

Engine code (5th digit)

Model year code (6th digit)

Example (1981 and later models):

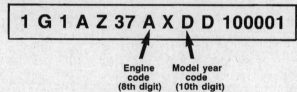

| 1 | G | 1 | A | Z | 37 | A | X | D | D | 100001 |

Engine code (8th digit)

Model year code (10th digit)

Model Year Codes

4 = 1974		B = 1981	
5 = 1975		C = 1982	
6 = 1976		D = 1983	
7 = 1977		E = 1984	
8 = 1978		F = 1985	
9 = 1979		G = 1986	
0 = 1980		H = 1987	
		J = 1988	
		K = 1989	
		L = 1990	
		M = 1991	
		N = 1992	
		P = 1993	
		R = 1994	

Engine codes

1974

A	4	140 (75 H.P.)
B	4	140 (85 H.P.)
C	6	250 (95 H.P.)
D	6	250 (100 H.P.)
H	8	350 (145 H.P.)
J	8	350 (195 H.P.)
K	8	350 (185 H.P.)
L	8	350 (160 H.P.)
R	8	400 (150 H.P.)
T	8	350 (245 H.P.)
U	8	400 (180 H.P.)
Y	8	454 (235 H.P.)
Z	8	454 (270 H.P.)

1975

A	4	140 (78 H.P.)
B	4	140 (87 H.P.)
C	6	250 (export)
D	6	250 (105 H.P.)
E	4	122
G	8	262
H	8	350 (145 H.P.)
J	8	350 (165 H.P.)
L	8	350 (155 H.P.)
T	8	350 (205 H.P.)
U	8	400
Y	8	454

1976

A	4	140 (70 H.P.)
B	4	140 (84 H.P.)
D	6	250
E	4	98
G	8	262
I	4	98
L	8	350 (165 H.P.)
O	4	122
Q	8	305
S	8	454

U	8	400
V	8	350 (145 H.P.)
X	8	350 (210 H.P.)

1977

B	4	140
D	6	250
E	4	98
I	4	85
L	8	350 (170 H.P.)
U	8	305
X	8	350 (210 H.P.)

1978

A	6	231
C	6	196
D	6	250
E	4	98 (63 H.P.)
H	8	350 (220 H.P.)
J	4	98 (68 H.P.)
L	8	350 (170 H.P.)
M	6	200
U	8	305
V	4	151 (exc Calif.)
I	4	141 (Calif.)

1979

A	6	231
C	6	196
D	6	250
E	4	98 (1 barrel)
G	8	305 (2 barrel)
H	8	305 (4 barrel)
J	8	267
L	8	350
M	6	200
O	4	98 (2 barrel)
V	4	151 (exc Calif.)
1	4	151 (Calif.)
2	6	231

4	8	350
8	8	350
9	4	151 (Calif.)

1980

A	6	231 (2 barrel)
H	8	305
J	8	267
K	6	229
L	8	350
N	8	350 (diesel)
V	4	151
3	6	231 (4 barrel)
5	4	151
6	8	350
7	6	173
8	8	350
9	4	98
0	4	98 (high output)

1981

A	6	231 (2 barrel)
D	4	111 (diesel)
H	8	305

Chevrolet (continued)

J	8	267
K	6	229
L	8	350
N	8	350 (diesel)
X	6	173
Z	6	173
3	6	231 (4 barrel)
5	4	151
6	8	350
9	4	98

1982

A	6	231
B	4	121
C	4	98
D	4	111 (diesel)
G	4	112
H	8	305
J	8	267
K	6	229
N	8	350 (diesel)
R	4	151
T	6	260 (diesel)
V	6	260 (diesel)
X	6	173
Z	6	173
1	6	173
2	4	151
7	8	305 (fuel injection)
8	8	350 (fuel injection)

1983

A	6	231
B	4	121 (export)
C	4	98
D	4	111 (diesel)
F	4	151 (export)
H	8	305
N	8	350 (diesel)
P	4	121
R	4	151
S	8	305
T	6	260 (diesel)
V	6	260 (diesel)
X	6	173
Z	6	173
1	6	173
2	4	151

5	4	151 (export)
6	8	350 (police)
7	8	305
8	8	350
9	6	229

1984

A	6	231
B	4	121 (export)
C	4	98
D	4	111 (diesel)
G	8	305
H	8	305
N	8	350 (diesel)
P	4	121
R	4	151
T	6	260 (diesel)
X	6	173
Z	6	173
1	6	173
2	4	151
6	8	350
8	8	350 (fuel injection)
9	6	229

1985 - 1986

A	6	231
C	4	98
D	4	111 (diesel)
F	8	305 (fuel injection)
G	8	305
H	8	305
N	8	350 (diesel)
P	4	121
R	4	151
S	6	173 (fuel injection)
T	6	260 (diesel)
W	6	173 (fuel injection)
X	6	173 (2 barrel)
Z	6	262
4	4	98
2	4	151
6	8	350 (police)
8	8	350 (fuel injection)

1987 - 1988

C	4	98 (2 barrel)
E	8	305 (fuel injection)
F	8	305 (TPI)
G	8	305 (4 barrel)

H	8	305 (4 barrel)
R	4	151 (TBI)
S	6	173 (MFI)
W	6	173 (MFI)
Y	8	305 (4 barrel)
Z	6	262 (TBI)
1	4	121 (TBI)
2	3	61 (fuel injection, turbocharged)
4	4	98 (2 barrel)
5	3	61
7	4	91
8	8	350 (TPI)
9	4	90 (fuel injection, turbocharged)

1989 - 1990

E	8	305 (fuel injection)
F	8	305 (fuel injection)
R	4	151 (fuel injection)
S	6	173 (fuel injection)
W	6	173 (fuel injection)
Y	8	305
1	4	121 (fuel injection)
8	8	350 (fuel injection)

1991 - 1992

7	8	350 (EFI)
8	8	350 (TPI)
A	4	138 (16V-MFI)
E	8	305 (EFI)
F	8	305 (TPI)
G	4	133 (MFI)
J	8	350 (MFI)
R	4	151 (EFI)
T	6	191 (MFI)
X	6	207 (MFI)

1993 - 1994

4	4	133 (MFI)
7	8	350 (EFI)
A	4	140 (MFI)
E	8	305 (EFI)
J	8	350 (EFI DOHC)
M	6	191 (SFI)
P	8	350 (MFI)
S	6	207 (SFI)
T	6	191 (MFI)
W	8	265 (SFI)
X	6	207 (MFI)

GENERAL MOTORS
Oldsmobile division

Example (1974 through 1980 models):

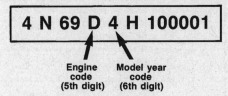

4 N 69 D 4 H 100001

Engine code (5th digit)
Model year code (6th digit)

Example (1981 and later models):

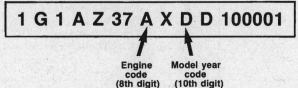

1 G 1 A Z 37 A X D D 100001

Engine code (8th digit)
Model year code (10th digit)

V.I.N. PLATE LOCATION

INSTRUMENT PANEL

Model Year Codes

4 = 1974		B = 1981	
5 = 1975		C = 1982	
6 = 1976		D = 1983	
7 = 1977		E = 1984	
8 = 1978		F = 1985	
9 = 1979		G = 1986	
0 = 1980		H = 1987	
		J = 1988	
		K = 1989	
		L = 1990	
		M = 1991	
		N = 1992	
		P = 1993	
		R = 1994	

Engine codes

1974

D	6	250
K	8	350 (180 H.P.)
M	8	350 (200 H.P.)
T	8	455 (210 H.P.)
U	8	455 (230 H.P.)
W	8	455 (230 H.P.)

1975

C	6	231
D	6	250
F	8	260
H	8	350 (145 H.P.)
J	8	350 (165 H.P.)
K	8	350 (170 H.P.)
R	8	400 (170 H.P.)
S	8	400 (185 H.P.)
T	8	455 (190 H.P.)
W	8	455 (215 H.P.)

1976

B	4	140
C	6	231
D	6	250
F	8	260
H	8	350
J	8	350
R	8	350
S	8	455
T	8	455

1977

A	6	231 (even firing)
B	4	140
C	6	231 (uneven firing)
F	8	260
G	8	350 (150 H.P.)
K	8	403
L	8	350 (170 H.P.)
R	8	350 (170 H.P.)
U	8	305

1978

A	6	231
F	8	260
H	8	305 (160 H.P.)
K	8	403
L	8	350 (170 H.P.)
N	8	350 (diesel)
R	8	350 (170 H.P.)
U	8	305 (145 H.P.)
V	4	151 (exc Calif.)
1	4	151 (Calif.)

1979

A	6	231
F	8	260
G	8	305 (2 barrel)
H	8	305 (4 barrel)
K	8	403
L	8	350
N	8	350 (diesel)
P	8	260 (diesel)
R	8	350
V	4	151 (exc Calif.)
Y	8	301
1	4	151 (Calif.)
2	6	231
9	4	151 (Calif.)

1980

A	6	231
F	8	260
H	8	305
N	8	350 (diesel)
R	8	350
V	4	151
Y	8	307
5	4	151
7	6	173

1981

A	6	231

F	8	260
N	8	350 (diesel)
X	6	173
Y	8	307
4	6	252
5	4	151

1982

A	6	231
B	4	121
E	6	181
G	4	112
N	8	350 (diesel)
R	4	151
T	6	260 (diesel)
V	6	260 (diesel)
X	6	173
Y	8	307
Z	6	173
4	6	252
8	8	260

1983

A	6	231
B	4	121 (export)
E	6	181
H	8	305 (export)

Oldsmobile (continued)

N	8	350 (diesel)
P	4	121
R	4	151
T	6	260 (diesel)
V	6	260 (diesel)
X	6	173
Y	8	307
Z	6	173
0	4	112
4	6	252
5	4	151 (export)
9	8	307

1984

A	6	231
B	4	121 (export)
E	6	181
H	8	305 (export)
N	8	350 (diesel)
P	4	121
R	4	151
T	6	260
V	6	260
X	6	173
Y	8	307
Z	6	173
0	4	112
3	6	231 (fuel injection)
4	6	252
9	8	307

1985 - 1986

A	6	231 (2 barrel)
B	6	231
E	6	181 (2 barrel)

H	8	305
L	6	181 (fuel injection)
N	8	350 (diesel)
P	4	121
R	4	151
T	6	260
U	4	151
W	6	173
X	6	173
Y	8	307
0	4	112
3	6	231 (fuel injection)
9	8	307

1987

A	6	231 (2 barrel)
K	4	122 (TBI)
L	6	181 (MFI)
R	4	151 (TBI)
U	4	151 (TBI)
W	6	173 (MFI)
Y	8	307 (4 barrel)
1	4	122 (TBI)
3	6	231 (SFI)
9	8	307 (4 barrel)

1988

B	6	231 (SFI)
C	6	231 (fuel injection)
D	4	140 (fuel injection)
K	4	122 (OHC)
L	6	181 (fuel injection)
R	4	151 (EFI)
U	4	151 (fuel injection)
W	6	173 (MFI)
Y	8	307 (4 barrel)
1	4	122 (EFI)

3	6	231 (SFI)
9	8	307

1989 - 1990

C	6	231 (fuel injection)
D	4	140 (fuel injection)
N	6	189 (fuel injection)
R	4	151 (fuel injection)
U	4	151 (fuel injection)
W	6	173 (fuel injection)
Y	8	307

1991 - 1992

1	6	231 (SFI)
7	8	350 (TBI)
A	4	140 (MFI)
C	6	231 (SFI)
D	4	140 (MFI)
E	8	305 (EFI)
L	6	231 (TPI)
N	6	204 (MFI)
R	4	151 (EFI)
T	6	141 (MFI)
U	4	151 (EFI)
X	6	207 (MFI)

1993 - 1994

1	6	231 (TPI supercharged)
3	4	140 (MFI)
4	4	133 (MFI)
A	4	140 (MFI)
D	4	140 (MFI)
L	6	231 (TPI)
M	6	191 (SFI)
N	6	204 (MFI)
T	6	191 (MFI)
X	6	207 (MFI)

GENERAL MOTORS
Pontiac division

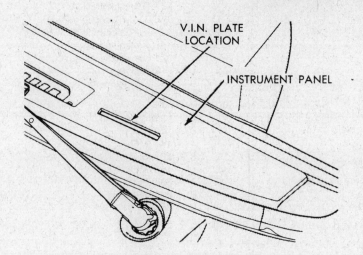

V.I.N. PLATE LOCATION

INSTRUMENT PANEL

Example (1974 through 1980 models):

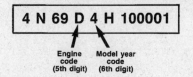

4 N 69 D 4 H 100001

Engine code (5th digit) Model year code (6th digit)

Example (1981 and later models):

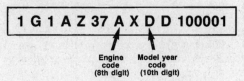

1 G 1 A Z 37 A X D D 100001

Engine code (8th digit) Model year code (10th digit)

Model Year Codes	
4 = 1974	B = 1981
5 = 1975	C = 1982
6 = 1976	D = 1983
7 = 1977	E = 1984
8 = 1978	F = 1985
9 = 1979	G = 1986
0 = 1980	H = 1987
	J = 1988
	K = 1989
	L = 1990
	M = 1991
	N = 1992
	P = 1993
	R = 1994

Engine codes

1974

D	6	250
J	8	350 (170 H.P.)
K	8	350 (200 H.P.)
M	8	350 (155 H.P.)
N	8	350 (170 H.P.)
P	8	400 (190 H.P.)
R	8	400 (175 H.P.)
S	8	400 (200 H.P.)
T	8	400 (225 H.P.)
W	8	455 (215 H.P.)
X	8	455 (290 H.P.)
Y	8	455 (250 H.P.)

1975

A	4	140 (78 H.P.)
B	4	140 (87 H.P.)
D	6	250
E	8	350 (175 H.P.)
F	8	260
H	8	350 (145 H.P.)
J	8	350 (165 H.P.)
M	8	350 (155 H.P.)
R	8	400 (170 H.P.)
S	8	400 (185 H.P.)
W	8	455

1976

A	4	140 (70 H.P.)
B	4	140 (84 H.P.)
C	6	231
D	6	250
F	8	260
H	8	350
J	8	350
M	8	350
N	8	400
P	8	350
W	8	455
Z	8	400

1977

A	6	231 (even firing)
B	4	140
C	6	231 (uneven firing)
K	8	403
L	8	350
P	8	350
R	8	350
U	8	305
V	4	151
Y	8	301
Z	8	400

1978

A	6	231
K	8	403
L	8	350
R	8	350
U	8	305
V	4	151 (exc Calif.)
W	8	301 (150 H.P.)
X	8	350
Y	8	301
Z	8	400
1	4	151 (Calif.)

1979

A	6	231
G	8	305
H	8	305
K	8	403
L	8	350
R	8	350
V	4	151 (exc Calif.)
W	8	301
X	8	350
Y	8	301
Z	8	400
1	4	151 (Calif.)
9	4	151 (Calif.)

1980

A	6	231
H	8	305
K	6	229
N	8	350 (diesel)
R	8	350
S	8	265
T	8	301 (turbo)
V	4	151
W	8	301
X	8	350
5	4	151
7	6	173

1981

A	6	231
G	4	112
H	8	305
N	8	350 (diesel)
S	8	260
T	8	301 (turbo)
W	8	301
X	6	173
Y	8	307
5	4	151
9	4	98

Pontiac (continued)

1982

A	6	231
C	4	98
G	4	112
N	8	350 (diesel)
R	4	151
T	6	260 (diesel)
X	6	173
Z	6	173
0	4	112
1	6	173
2	4	151
4	6	252
7	8	305

1983

A	6	231
B	4	121 (export)
C	4	98
D	4	111 (diesel)
F	4	151 (export)
H	8	305
L	6	173
N	8	350 (diesel)
P	4	121
R	4	151
S	8	305
T	6	260 (diesel)
X	6	173
Z	6	173
0	4	112
1	6	173
2	4	151
5	4	151 (export)
9	6	229

1984

A	6	231
B	4	121 (export)
C	4	98
D	4	111 (diesel)
G	8	305
H	8	305
J	4	112
L	6	173
N	8	350 (diesel)
P	4	121
R	4	151
T	6	260 (diesel)
X	6	173
Z	6	173
0	4	112
1	6	173
2	4	151

1985 - 1986

A	6	231
C	4	98
D	4	111 (diesel)
F	8	305 (fuel injection)
G	8	305
H	8	305
J	4	112
L	6	173
N	8	350 (diesel)
P	4	121
R	4	151
S	6	173 (fuel injection)
T	6	260 (diesel)
U	4	151
W	6	173 (fuel injection)
X	6	173 (2 barrel)
Y	8	307
Z	6	262
0	4	112
2	4	151
9	6	173 (fuel injection)

1987

A	6	231 (2 barrel)
C	4	98 (2 barrel)
F	8	305 (TPI)
H	8	305 (4 barrel)
K	4	122 (TBI)
L	6	181 (MFI)
M	4	122 (MFI, turbocharged)
R	4	151 (TBI)
S	6	173 (MFI)
U	4	151 (TBI)
W	6	173 (MFI)
Y	8	307 (4 barrel)
Z	6	262 (TBI)
3	6	231 (SFI)
6	4	98 (fuel injection)
8	8	350 (TPI)
9	6	170 (MFI)

1988

B	6	231 (SFI)
C	6	231 (fuel injection)
D	4	140 (16V)
E	8	305 (fuel injection)
F	8	305 (MFI)
H	8	305 (4 barrel)
K	4	122 (EFI)
M	4	122 (turbocharged, MFI)
R	4	152 (EFI)
S	6	170 (MFI)
T	6	189 (fuel injection)
U	4	152 (EFI)

W	6	170 (MFI)
Y	8	305
3	6	231 (SFI)
6	4	98 (EFI)
8	8	350 (fuel injection)
9	6	170 (fuel injection)

1989 - 1990

C	6	231
D	4	140 (DOHC)
E	8	305 (fuel injection)
F	8	305 (fuel injection)
K	4	121 (fuel injection)
M	4	181 (fuel injection, turbocharged)
R	4	151 (fuel injection)
S	6	173 (fuel injection)
T	6	189 (fuel injection
U	4	151 (fuel injection)
W	6	173 (fuel injection)
Y	8	307
6	4	98 (fuel injection)
8	8	350 (fuel injection)

1991 - 1992

6	4	98 (EFI)
8	8	350 (TPI)
A	4	138 (MFI)
C	6	231 (SFI)
D	4	138 (MFI)
F	8	305 (TPI)
H	4	121 (MFI)
H	8	305 (EFI)
K	4	121 (EFI)
N	6	204 (MFI)
S	6	191 (MFI)
T	6	191 (EFI)
U	4	151 (EFI)
V	6	191 (MFI)
X	6	207 (MFI)

1993 - 1994

1	6	231 (TPI supercharged)
3	4	140 (MFI)
6	4	98 (EFI)
A	4	140 (MFI)
D	4	140 (MFI)
H	4	121 (MFI)
L	6	231 (TPI)
N	6	204 (MFI)
P	8	350 (MFI)
S	6	204 (SFI)
T	6	191 (MFI)
V	6	191 (MFI)
X	6	207 (MFI)

CHEVROLET, GMC, OLDSMOBILE & PONTIAC Light trucks

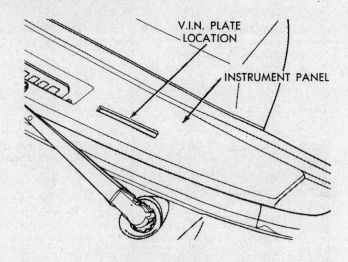

V.I.N. PLATE LOCATION

INSTRUMENT PANEL

MFD. BY GENERAL MOTORS CORPORATION

GVWR

GAWR FRONT ☐   GAWR REAR ☐

VIN ☐

CAMPER LOADING DATA

CWR ☐   DIM A ☐   DIM B ☐

INFLATION DATA FOR TIRES FURNISHED WITH VEHICLE

FRONT ☐   PRESSURE ☐
REAR ☐   PRESSURE ☐

WARRANTY VOIDED IF LOADED IN EXCESS OF RATINGS ☐
SEE OWNERS MANUAL FOR OTHER LOADING AND INFLATION DATA

Typical plate found on driver's door pillar
(1974 — 1980 models)

Example (1974 through 1980 models):

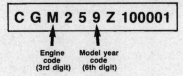

C G M 2 5 9 Z 100001

Engine code (3rd digit)   Model year code (6th digit)

Example (1981 and later models):

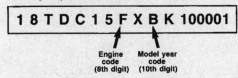

1 8 T D C 1 5 F X B K 100001

Engine code (8th digit)   Model year code (10th digit)

Model Year Codes

4 = 1974	B = 1981	J = 1988
5 = 1975	C = 1982	K = 1989
6 = 1976	D = 1983	L = 1990
7 = 1977	E = 1984	M = 1991
8 = 1978	F = 1985	N = 1992
9 = 1979	G = 1986	P = 1993
0 = 1980	H = 1987	R = 1994

Engine codes

1974

L	8	454 (245 H.P.)
P	6	250 (export)
Q	6	250
S	6	292 (LP gas)
T	6	292
U	8	350 (export)
V	8	350 (2 barrel)
W	8	350 (LP gas)
Y	8	350 (160 H.P.)
Z	8	454 (230 H.P.)

1975

L	8	454 (245 H.P.)
M	8	400
P	6	250 (export)
Q	6	250
R	6	292 (export)
T	6	292
U	8	350 (export)
V	8	350 (2 barrel)
Y	8	350 (4 barrel)
Z	8	454 (230 H.P.)

1976

D	6	250
L	8	350
S	8	454
T	6	292
U	8	400
V	8	350
Y	8	454

1977 - 1980

D	6	250
G	8	305
L	8	350
M	8	350
P	8	350
R	8	400
S	8	454
T	6	292
U	8	305
W	8	454
X	8	400
Y	8	454
Z	8	350 (diesel)

1981

A	6	231
D	6	250
F	8	305
G	8	305
H	8	305
J	8	267
K	6	229

L	8	350
M	8	350
N	4	110
P	8	350
T	6	292
W	8	454
Z	8	350 (diesel)

1982 - 1984

A	4	119
B	6	173
C	8	379 (diesel)
D	6	250
F	8	305
H	8	305
J	8	379 (diesel)
L	8	350
M	8	350
N	4	111
P	8	350
S	4	134 (diesel)
T	6	292
W	8	454
Y	4	121

1985 - 1986

A	4	119
B	6	173
C	8	379 (diesel)

Chevrolet, GMC, Oldsmobile & Pontiac Light trucks (continued)

E	4	151
F	8	305
H	8	305
J	8	379 (diesel)
K	8	350
L	8	350
M	8	350
N	8	263
R	6	173
S	4	133 (diesel)
T	6	292
W	8	454
Z	6	262

1987

B	6	173 (fuel injection)
C	8	379 (diesel)
E	4	151 (TBI)
H	8	305 (TBI)
J	8	379 (diesel)
K	8	350 (TBI)
M	8	350 (4 barrel)
N	8	454 (TBI)
R	6	173 (TBI)
T	6	292 (1 barrel)
W	8	454 (4 barrel)
Z	6	262 (TBI)

1988

B	6	173 (fuel injection)
C	8	379 (diesel)
E	4	151 (TBI)
H	8	305 (fuel injection)
J	8	379 (diesel)
K	8	350 (fuel injection)
N	8	454 (fuel injection)
Z	6	262 (fuel injection)

1989 - 1990

C	8	379 (diesel)
E	4	151 (fuel injection)
H	8	305 (fuel injection)
J	8	379 (diesel)
K	8	350 (fuel injection)
M	8	350
N	8	454 (fuel injection)
R	6	173 (fuel injection)
W	8	454
Z	6	262 (fuel injection)

1991 - 1992 Chevrolet/GMC

A	4	151 (EFI)
B	6	262 (EFI)
C	8	379 (diesel)
E	4	151 (EFI)
H	8	305 (EFI)
J	8	379 (diesel)
K	8	350 (EFI)
M	8	350 (4 barrel)
N	8	454 (EFI)
R	6	173 (EFI)
W	8	454 (4 barrel)
Z	6	262 (EFI)

1991 - 1992 Oldsmobile

D	6	191 (EFI)
L	6	231 (TPI)

W	6	262 (EFI)
Z	6	262 (TBI)

1991 - 1992 Pontiac

C	6	231 (SFI)
D	6	191 (EFI)

1993 - 1994 Chevrolet/GMC

4	4	133 (MFI)
A	4	151 (EFI)
C	8	379 (diesel)
D	6	191 (EFI)
F	8	400 (turbo diesel)
H	8	305 (EFI)
J	8	379 (diesel)
K	8	350 (EFI)
K	8	350 (EFI)
L	8	231 (SFI)
N	8	454 (EFI)
P	8	400 (diesel)
R	6	173 (EFI)
S	8	400 (turbo diesel)
W	6	262 (CPI)
Z	6	262 (EFI)

1993 - 1994 Oldsmobile

D	6	189 (TBI)
L	6	231 (TPI)
W	6	262 (CPI)

1993 - 1994 Pontiac

C	6	231 (SFI)
D	6	189 (EFI)

DODGE/PLYMOUTH Light trucks

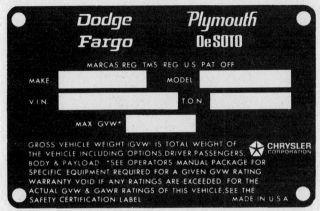

Typical plate found on driver's door pillar
(1974 — 1980 models)

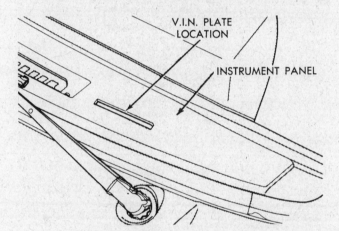

Example (1974 through 1980 models):

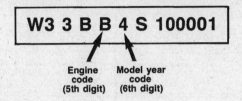

W3 3 B B 4 S 100001

Engine code (5th digit) — Model year code (6th digit)

Example (1981 and later models):

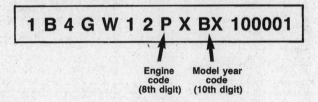

1 B 4 G W 1 2 P X BX 100001

Engine code (8th digit) — Model year code (10th digit)

Model Year Codes

4 = 1974	B = 1981	J = 1988
5 = 1975	C = 1982	K = 1989
6 = 1976	D = 1983	L = 1990
7 = 1977	E = 1984	M = 1991
8 = 1978	F = 1985	N = 1992
9 = 1979	G = 1986	P = 1993
0 = 1980	H = 1987	R = 1994

Engine codes

1974

A	8	440
B	6	225
C	6	225
D	8	440
E	8	318
F	8	360
G	8	318
J	8	400
K	8	360
L	8	360
M	8	361
P	8	413
T	8	360
X	6	(special order)
Y	8	(special order)

1975 - 1977

A	8	440
B	6	225
C	6	225
D	8	440
E	8	318
F	8	360
G	8	318
J	8	400
K	8	360
L	8	361
M	8	361
P	8	413
R	8	413
X	6	(special order)
Y	8	(special order)

1978 - 1980

A	8	440
B	6	225
C	6	225
D	8	440
E	8	318
F	8	360
G	8	318
H	6	243 (diesel)
J	8	400
K	8	360
N	6	225
P	8	318
R	8	413
S	8	360 (high performance)
T	8	360 V8 (special order)
X	6	(special order)
Y	8	(special order)

1981 - 1982

E	6	225
P	8	318
R	8	318
S	8	360
T	8	360
U	8	360 (heavy duty)
V	8	360 (heavy duty)
W	6	225

1983 - 1984

H	6	225
M	6	225
N	6	225 (special)
T	8	318
U	8	318
V	8	360
W	8	360 (exc Calif.)

1985 - 1986

H	6	225
I	8	360
T	8	318
V	8	360
W	8	360

Dodge/Plymouth Light trucks (continued)

1987 1988

C	4	135 (2 barrel)
H	6	225 (1 barrel)
M	6	239 (2 barrel)
T	8	318 (2 barrel)
W	8	360 (4 barrel)
1	8	360 (4 barrel, California)
3	6	187

1989 - 1990

D	4	122

G	4	153
J	4	153
K	4	153
S	6	181
X	6	239
Y	8	318
3	6	187
5	8	360
7	8	360
8	6	360 (diesel)

1991 - 1992

3	6	181 (MFI)
8	6	360 (turbo diesel)
C	6	360 (turbo diesel)
G	4	153 (EFI)
K	4	153 (EFI)
R	6	202 (MFI)

W	4	143 (MPI)
X	6	239 (MFI)
Y	8	318 (MFI)
Z	8	360 (EFI)

1993 - 1994

3	6	181 (MFI)
C	6	360 (turbo diesel)
E	10	488 (MFI)
G	4	144 (MFI)
G	4	153 (EFI)
K	4	153 (EFI)
L	6	231 (MFI)
R	6	202 (MFI)
X	6	239 (MFI)
Y	8	318 (MFI)
Z	8	360 (MFI)

FORD Light trucks

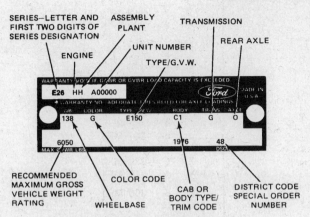

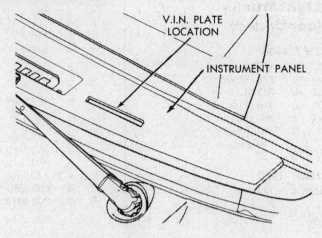

Typical plate found on driver's door pillar
(1974 — 1980 models)

Model year codes

001 - V00000 = 1974
V0001 - W20000, Econoline = 1974
      exc. Econoline = 1975
W20001 - X60000 = 1975
A00001 - D25000 = 1976
O00001 - X80000 = 1977
X80001 - Z25000, exc. Bronco = 1977
                 Bronco = 1978
AE0001 - CK9999, exc. Bronco = 1978
DC0001 - FK9000 = 1979
GA0001 - KE9999 = 1980

4 = 1974	B = 1981
5 = 1975	C = 1982
6 = 1976	D = 1983
7 = 1977	E = 1984
8 = 1978	F = 1985
9 = 1979	G = 1986
0 = 1980	H = 1987
	J = 1988
	K = 1989
	L = 1990
	M = 1991
	N = 1992
	P = 1993
	R = 1994

Example (1974 through 1980 models):

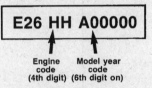

Engine code (4th digit)   Model year code (6th digit on)

Example (1981 and later models):

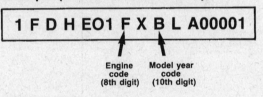

Engine code (8th digit)   Model year code (10th digit)

Engine codes

1974

A	6	240
B	6	300
G	8	302
H	8	390
J	8	460
Y	8	360
1	6	240
5	8	360

1975 - 1976

A	8	460 (Econoline)
9	6	300
G	8	302
H	8	351 (Econoline)
	8	390 (exc. Econoline)
J	8	460
M	8	390
Y	8	360
1	6	240 (special order)

1977 - 1979

A	8	460
B	6	300
G	8	302
H	8	351
J	8	460
K	6	300 (heavy duty)
S	8	400
Z		(special order)

1980

E	6	300
F	8	302
G	8	351 (non-lead fuel)
L	8	460
W	8	351 (leaded fuel)
Z	8	400
0		(special order)
7	8	351 (export)

1981 - 1982

D	8	255
E	6	300
F	8	302
G	8	351
L	8	460
Z	8	400
7	8	351
9	6	300

1983 - 1984

A	4	140
C	4	122
F	8	302
G	8	351
L	8	460
P	4	134 (diesel)
S	6	170
Y	6	300
1	8	426 (diesel)
3	6	230

1985 - 1986

A	4	140
C	4	122
E	4	143 (turbo diesel)
F	8	302
G	8	351
H	8	351
L	8	460
N	8	302
S	6	171
T	6	179
U	6	183
Y	6	300
1	8	421 (diesel)

Ford Light trucks (continued)

1987

A	4	140 (MFI)
C	4	122 (1 barrel)
E	4	140 (turbo diesel)
H	8	351 (4 barrel)
L	8	460 (4 barrel)
N	8	302 (EFI)
T	6	177 (EFI)
U	6	183 (EFI)
Y	6	300 (EFI)
1	8	426 (diesel)
9	6	300 (LPG)

1988

A	4	140 (EFI)
C	4	122 (2 barrel)
G	8	460 (EFI)

H	8	351 (EFI)
M	8	445 (diesel)
N	8	302 (EFI)
T	6	177 (EFI)
U	6	183 (EFI)
Y	6	300 (EFI)

1989 - 1990

A	4	140
C	4	122
G	8	460
H	8	351
N	8	302
S	6	300
T	6	179
U	6	182
Y	6	300
M	8	444 (diesel)

1991 - 1992

A	4	140 (EFI)

G	8	460 (EFI)
H	8	351 (EFI)
M	8	444 (diesel)
N	8	302 (EFI)
T	6	179 (EFI)
U	6	182 (EFI)
X	6	244 (EFI)
Y	6	300 (EFI)

1993 - 1994

A	4	140 (EFI)
G	8	460 (EFI)
H	8	351 (EFI)
K	8	444 (turbo diesel)
M	8	444 (diesel)
N	8	302 (EFI)
R	8	351 (EFI)
U	6	245 (EFI)
X	6	244 (EFI)
Y	6	300 (EFI)

JEEP

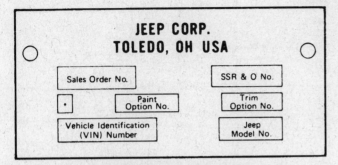

JEEP CORP.
TOLEDO, OH USA

Sales Order No.

SSR & O No.

Paint Option No.

Trim Option No.

Vehicle Identification (VIN) Number

Jeep Model No.

Typical plate found under the hood
or on left side of instrument panel

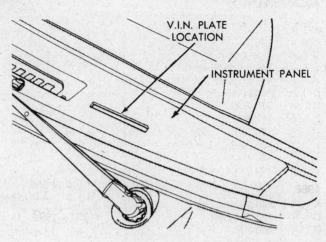

V.I.N. PLATE LOCATION

INSTRUMENT PANEL

Example (1974 through 1980 models):

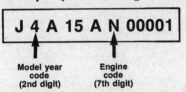

J 4 A 15 A N 00001

Model year code (2nd digit)

Engine code (7th digit)

Example (1981 and later models):

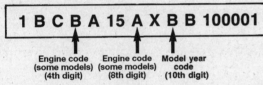

1 B C B A 15 A X B B 100001

Engine code (some models) (4th digit)

Engine code (some models) (8th digit)

Model year code (10th digit)

Model Year Codes

4 = 1974	B = 1981	J = 1988
5 = 1975	C = 1982	K = 1989
6 = 1976	D = 1983	L = 1990
7 = 1977	E = 1984	M = 1991
8 = 1978	F = 1985	N = 1992
9 = 1979	G = 1986	P = 1993
0 = 1980	H = 1987	R = 1994

Engine codes

1974

A	6	258
E	6	232
H	8	304
N	8	360
P	8	360
Z	8	401

1975 - 1976

A	6	258
E	6	232
H	8	304
N	8	360
P	8	360
Z	8	401

1977 - 1980

A	6	258
B	4	151
C	6	258
E	6	232
H	8	304
N	8	360
P	8	360
Z	8	401

1981 - 1983

B	4	151
C	6	258
F	4	145 (diesel)
H	8	304
L	6	232
N	8	360
U	4	151

1984

C	6	258
N	8	360
U	4	151
W	6	173
Y	4	151 (export)

1985 - 1986

B	4	124 (diesel)
C	6	258
H	4	150
N	8	360
U	4	150
W	6	173

1987

B	4	126 (turbo diesel)
C	6	258 (2 barrel)
H	4	150 (TBI)
M	6	242 (MFI)
N	8	360 (2 barrel)

1988

C	6	258 (2 barrel)
H	4	150 (TBI)
M	6	242 (EFI)
N	8	360 (2 barrel)

1989 - 1990

E	4	150
L	6	242
T	6	258

1991 - 1992

7	8	360 (2V carb)
P	4	150 (MFI)
S	6	242 (MFI)
V	6	242 (MFI)

1993 - 1994

P	4	150 (MFI)
S	6	242 (MFI)
Y	8	318 (MFI)

Notes

_____

_____

_____

_____

_____

_____

_____

_____

_____

_____

_____

_____

_____

_____

_____

_____

Appendix B
Glossary
of used car terms

20K - 20,000 miles on odometer. Sometimes seen as "20M" for 20,000 miles. In car prices, the K or M are also used for "thousands" of dollars, as in "best offer over $15K".

ABS - Anti-Lock Braking System.

A/C - Air-conditioning.

Airbag - Also listed as SRS by manufacturers, for Supplemental Restrain System, which is an airbag mounted inside the steering wheel that inflates to protect the driver in a crash. A vehicle with dual airbags has one for the driver and one for a front-seat passenger.

Alarm - Vehicle is equipped with a burglar alarm of some type, which could be simple or elaborate.

Alloys - Aftermarket custom aluminum wheels.

AM/FM - refers to a basic radio. "AM/FM/cass" usually refers to a combination radio and tape player.

As is - Vehicle probably has some cosmetic or mechanical defects, but the owner doesn't want to fix them and he isn't guaranteeing the vehicle is perfect.

AT, A/T or auto - Automatic transmission.

AWD - All-Wheel-Drive, an expensive version of four-wheel-drive, designed for superior road handling, not off-roading.

Base model - A stripper. Few extras.

Bedliner - On pickups, a plastic insert that protects the bed from dings and dirt.

B/O - Best offer, as in "B/O over 15K".

Cass - Stereo cassette tape player.

CD - Compact-Disc music system.

Cell - Vehicle has a cellular phone installed.

Cherry - Excellent condition.

Clean - Usually a well-kept car in very good condition, though one person's "good" is another's mediocre.

Clear title - When the owner has no outstanding liens against the vehicle and is free to sell it himself. If only the registered owner is listed on the title certificate, the vehicle is generally said to have clear title.

Clip - A car made from the intact front end of one wreck and the rear of another.

Compact - A car with a 100 to 105 inch wheelbase and an overall length of 175 to 185 inches (see also Subcompact).

Cnvrt, or Convert. - A convertible, with a folding soft top, also called a "ragtop" in slang terms.

Cpe - A coupe, which is a two-door vehicle with a hard top.

Crm Puff - Cream puff, an example so perfect it seems never to have been driven.

Cruise - Equipped with cruise control, also listed as CC.

Demo - Usually one-year-old or less, used by "dealership staff".

Dly Driv - A claim that the vehicle is driven daily, the implication being that the car is trouble-free.

Divorce forces sale - The owner could be going through a rough time and the car may be a bargain price, or he could be pulling your leg.

Estate Sale - Usually means the owner has died, and someone else is selling the car for the family.

Ext. warr. - Has an extended warranty of some sort, which might be transferable to the next owner (see Chapter 1).

Fac. - Factory-installed accessory, as in "fac AC".

Fact. warr. - Has a factory warranty, which might be transferable to the next owner (see Chapter 1).

Firm - The listed price is not open to bargaining (however, many sellers turn out to be more flexible in the end).

Flat spot - A momentary lapse in power as an engine is accelerating.

Full pwr, Loaded, All opts - Equipped with all the common power accessories such as power steering, brakes and windows. Usually more expensive than a strippo. Also listed sometimes as "F/power".

Full-size - A car with a wheelbase over 110 inches and overall length of over 195 inches.

Full-size spare - The spare tire on the vehicle is full-size, not a temporary "space-saver" spare.

Fully independent suspension - Each wheel has its own suspension, independent of the other front or rear wheel.

4dr - Vehicle in question has four doors, as opposed to one with two doors (usually listed as 2dr).

FWD - Front wheel drive.

4WD - Four-wheel-drive, also listed as 4x4.

Gar kept - Garage kept; if true, this generally means that the car is in above-average condition.

Gd transp. - Good transportation; may be in acceptable running condition but is probably otherwise dilapidated.

Hatchback - A car without a trunk. The rear window, and sometimes a portion of the body below the window as well, are hinged at the top so that the entire assembly can swing up and out of the way in order to load or unload the car (also known as a *liftback*). Also seen abbreviated as HB.

Hi Miles - Means the vehicle has above-average mileage on the odometer, and the owner is being up-front about it.

Hwy miles - Meaning that most of the vehicle's mileage has been accumulated on the highway. Conventional wisdom is that highway mileage is less damaging to the car than the same mileage accumulated in the city.

ID'd - Means the car has an anti-theft system in which various parts of the car are marked with a nationally-recorded code number to discourage theft. A dealer option usually found on high-end vehicles.

Independent suspension - The wheels are not connected to one another. A disturbance at one wheel has little effect on the other wheel, which makes for better ride and handling.

Keyless entry - A security/convenience option on luxury cars, where vehicle entry is made with a "beeper" on your keychain or by pushing code buttons on the car door.

Knock - A term used to describe various noises in an engine made by loose or worn mechanical parts, preignition, detonation, etc.

Lthr - Leather interior.

Liftback - See *hatchback*.

Lo mi - Low mileage; generally good news, but a car that's spent most of its life making short trips may have exhausted more of its useful miles than one driven frequently on the highway.

Lug Rck - Luggage rack, usually an option only on station wagons and sport utility vehicles.

Mechanic's dream, handyman's special - Euphemisms for a car sure to need much attention.

Mid-size - A car with a 105 to 110 inch wheelbase and an overall length of 185 to 200 inches.

Mint - Like-new condition; if true, price will likely be high.

Mnrf - Moonroof, which is similar to a sunroof. Many people use the terms interchangeably. Officially though, a *sunroof* is metal and slides open to expose you to air and sun, while a *moonroof* is glass and may not open at all, but has an interior, cloth shade that can be slid across inside to keep out the sun.

MPG - Miles per gallon, a measure of fuel economy.

MSRP - Manufacturer's Suggested Retail Price, usually used only in dealer ads.

Must see to appreciate - Suggests either a price far out of line or a truly superior example.

Glossary of used car terms

Must sell, Sacrifice - Examine carefully; the owner may really be moving out of town or could be trying to unload a lemon.

Needs work - Look at one of these only if you're mechanically inclined (and adept).

New paint - How much body work does it cover up, and why would it be needed on a late-model vehicle?

No rust - Remember that the most serious rusting could be on the car's underside.

Non-smkr - Is the car or its owner a non-smoker? Good news either way.

Nu tags - The vehicle has recently had its annual inspection and/or the registration has been renewed and is good for another year. Buying a car with tags just about to expire means **you** will shortly be paying that expense.

OAC - On approval of credit. Usually listed in dealership ads, it means that the advertised price and terms are as stated, **if** you have a good-enough credit rating.

OBO - Or best offer; owner has little hope of getting the asking price. Also listed as "BO $XXXX" or "best offer over $XXXXX".

One owner, orig owner - As a rule, the best car to get, provided the sole owner has been a careful one. Check the title.

OWC - This means the owner is willing to carry (owner will carry) some kind of finance contract, in which you pay something down on the vehicle and you agree to pay the rest in a lump or in periodic payments.

Passenger capacity - The EPA rates capacity by the number of seat belts installed. But some cars with six seat belts might really only hold five adults, or even four, in real comfort.

PB, PS - Power brakes and power steering.

PDL, PL - Power door locks.

P seat - -Power seat.

Priced to sell - A classic car-ad line, meaning that, in the seller's opinion, this is a great deal, and less than the going rate.

Private, private party - Private seller. Remember, some shady professional dealers represent themselves as private sellers in classified ads. Also abbreviated as PP.

Program car - Another name for a demo.

Ragtop - Slang term for a convertible.

Rblt. - Usually refers to a rebuilt engine or transmission. Should be a cause for suspicion on a late-model vehicle.

Reconditioning - Before being put on the lot, a car has its body cleaned and waxed, its engine degreased and detailed, the interior de-stained and shampooed, flawed parts repaired or replaced, and paint retouched. Mechanical work, however, is not usually a part of the reconditioning process.

Records - Implies that the seller has all the receipts and maintenance records for everything he claims has been rebuilt or renewed on the vehicle. Also listed as "all rcpts" or all receipts.

Rims - Aftermarket custom wheels.

Rstrd - Restored, usually seen in reference to older vehicles. Everyone's definition of "restored" varies from a simple repaint to a body-off-frame restoration.

Runs good - Probably doesn't look too good.

RV - Recreational vehicle, which could be anything from a small camper shell on a mini-truck to a huge, bus-like motorhome.

RWD - Rear wheel drive.

Sale or trade - Means the owner will take cash payment for the car or take in something else of value he wants, as in "For Sale or trade for boat and trailer". Some private-party sellers will take part cash, part-trade.

Semi-independent suspension - The front wheels are fully independent but the rear wheels are connected by a solid axle.

Shell - Small camper-shell cover on the bed of a pick-up.

Shwrm - The claim is that the vehicle is in "showroom" condition, i.e. that it is as nice as when it sat new in a dealer showroom.

Smogged - In states that have annual or biannual smog inspections, this means the vehicle in question has just had its test and passed.

Spinner - Slang term for a seller who turns back an odometer to falsify the true mileage of a vehicle.

Stick - A stick shift, or manual transmission. Also abbreviated as Stk, as in "4-spd stk".

Stripper, strippo - Bottom-of-the-line model. No accessories other than a heater and, maybe, a radio.

Subcompact - A car with a wheelbase under 100 inches and an overall length of less than 175 inches.

Sunroof - This covers a variety of accessories, from factory-installed, electrically-powered sunroofs to inexpensive, owner-installed sunroofs that may tilt up slightly but don't open. The value of this option varies with the type.

Tilt - Has tilt steering column.

Tilt/Tele - A steering column that telescopes as well as tilts, changing length and driving angle.

Tint - The windows have been tinted.

T-top - The vehicle has easily removable roof sections (usually two) that give an open-air, semi-convertible feeling.

Wgn - Station wagon.

Winch - An optional pulling device (with a cable) on the front bumper of a vehicle, usually a four-wheel-drive, used to pull the parent vehicle or another out of a stuck situation while off-roading.

Appendix C
Helpful resources

Automobile manufacturers

Acura Division, American Honda Motor Co.
1919 Torrance Blvd.
Torrance, CA 90501-2746
Phone: (310) 783-2000 Fax (310) 783-3900

Alfa Romeo Distributors of North America
8259 Exchange Drive.
P.O. Box 598026
Orlando, FL 32859-8026
Phone: (407) 856-5000 Fax: (407)856-5075

Aston Martin Lagonda of North America, Inc.
1290 East Main Street
Stamford, CT 06902
Phone: (203) 359-2259 Fax: (203)

Audi of America, Inc.
3800 Hamlin Road
Auburn Hills, MI 48326
Phone: (810) 340-5000 Fax: (810) 340-5150

Automobiles Citroen
62 Blvd. Victor Hugo
Neuilly sur Seine
922089 Cedex, France
Phone: (33) 1 47483300 Fax: (33) 47484068

BMW of North America, Inc.
300 Chestnut Ridge Rd.
Woodcliff Lake, NJ 07675
Phone: (201) 307-4000 Fax: (201) 307-4045

Buick Motor Division
General Motors
902 East Hamilton Avenue
Flint, MI 48550
Phone: (810) 236-5000

Cadillac Motor Division
General Motors
Building 2-6
30009 Van Dyke Avenue
Warren, MI 48090
Phone: (810) 492-4329 Fax: (810) 492-4330

Chevrolet Motor Division
General Motors
30007 Van Dyke Avenue
Warren, MI 48090
Phone: (810) 492-8841

Automobile manufacturers
(continued)

Chrysler Corp.
12000 Chrysler Dr.
Highland Park, MI 48288-1919
Phone: (313) 956-5741

Chrysler Canada, Ltd.
2450 Chrysler Centre
Windsor, Ontario, Canada N9A 4H6
Phone: (519) 973-2000 Fax: (519) 973-2980

Dihatsu America, Inc.
4422 Corporate Center Drive
Los Alamitos, CA 90720
Phone: (714) 761-7000 Fax: (714) 952-3197

Fiat Auto U.S.A. Inc.
375 Park Avenue, Ste. 2703
New York, NY 10152-0082
Phone: (212) 207-0947 Fax: (212) 421-5194

Ford Motor Co.
The American Road
Dearborn, MI 48121
Phone: (313) 322-3000

Ford Motor Co. of Canada, Ltd.
The Canadian Road
Oakville, Ontario, Canada L6J 5E4
Phone: (905) 845-2511

General Motors Corp.
General Motors Bldg.
3044 W. Grand Blvd.
Detroit, MI 48202
Phone: (313) 556-5000

General Motors of Canada Ltd.
1908 Colonel Sam Dr.
Oshawa, Ontario, Canada L1H 8P7
Phone: (416) 644-5000

GMC Truck Division
General Motors
31 Judson Street
Pontiac, MI 48342
Phone: (810) 456-5000

Honda Division, American Honda Motor Co.
1919 Torrance Boulevard
Torrance, CA 90501-2746
Phone: (310) 783-2000 Fax: (310) 783-3900

Hyundai Motor America
10550 Talbert Ave.
Fountain Valley, CA 92728
Phone: (714) 965-3508 Fax: (714) 965-3816

Hyundai Auto Canada Inc.
75 Frontenac Dr.
Markham, Ontario, Canada L3R 6H2
Phone: (416) 477-0202 Fax (416) 477-0187

Infiniti Division, Nissan Motor Corp. in U.S.A.
18501 S. Figueroa Street
Carson, CA 90248-6405
Phone: (310) 532-3111 Fax: (310) 719-3343

American Isuzu Motors, Inc.
2300 Pellisier Place
Whittier, CA 90601
Phone: (310) 699-0500 Fax: (310) 692-7135

Jaguar Cars Inc.
555 MacArthur Blvd.
Mahwah, NH 07430
Phone: (201) 818-8500 Fax: (201) 818-9770

KIA Motors America, Inc.
P. O. Box 52410
Irvine, CA 92619-2410
Phone: (714) 470-7000 Fax: (714) 470-2800

Lexus Division, Toyota Motor Sales U.S.A.
19001 S. Western Avenue
Torrance, CA 90509
Phone: (310) 328-2075

Lincoln-Mercury Division
Ford Motor Co.
300 Renaissance Center
Detroit, MI 48243
Phone: (313) 446-4450 Fax: (313) 446-5899

Mazda Motor of America Inc.
7755 Irvine Center Drive
Irvine, CA 92630
Phone: (714) 727-1990 Fax (714) 727-6813

Mercedes-Benz of North America Inc.
1 Mercedes Drive
Montvale, NJ 07645-0350
Phone: (201) 573-2246 Fax: (201) 573-4370

Mitsubishi Motor Sales of America Inc.
6400 Katella Ave.
Cypress, CA 90630
Phone: (714) 372-6000 Fax: (714) 373-1020

Nissan North America Inc.
990 W. 190th St.
Torrance, CA 90502
Phone: (213) 768-3700 Fax: (213) 327-2272

Nissan Canada Inc.
5290 Orbitor Dr.
Mississauga, Ontario, L4W 4Z5
Phone: (905) 629-2888 Fax: (905) 629-9742

Oldsmobile Division
General Motors
920 Townsend Street
Lansing, MI 48921
Phone: (517) 377-5000

Peugeot Motors of America Inc.
1 Peugeot Plaza
Lyndhurst, NJ 07071
Phone: (201) 935-8400

Pontiac Division
General Motors
1 Pontiac Plaza
Pontiac, MI 48340
Phone: (810) 857-5000

Porsche Cars North America Inc.
100 W. Liberty St.
Reno, NV 89501
Phone: (702) 348-3000 Fax: (702) 348-3770

Range Rover of North America Inc.
4390 Parliament Place
P.O. Box 1503
Lanham, MD 20706
Phone: (301) 731-9040 Fax: (301) 731-9054

Renault U.S.A. Inc.
4000 Town Center
Suite 480
Southfield, MI 48075
Phone: (810) 358-8800 Fax: (810) 358-4382

SAAB Cars U.S.A., Inc.
P.O. Box 9000
Norcross, GA 30091
Phone: (404) 279-0100 Fax: (404) 279-6582

Saturn Corp.
General Motors
P. O. Box 7025
Troy, MI 48007-7025
Phone: (810) 524-5000 Fax: (810) 528-6300

Subaru of America Inc.
Subaru Plaza
P.O. Box 6000
Cherry Hill, NJ 08034-6000
Phone: (609) 488-8500 Fax: (609) 488-0485

American Suzuki Motor Corp.
3251 Imperial Highway
Brea, CA 92621
Phone: (714) 996-7040 Fax: (714) 524-2512

Toyota Motor Sales U.S.A. Inc.
19001 S. Western Ave.
Torrance, CA 90509
Phone: (310) 618-4000 Fax: (310) 619-7800

Volkswagen of America Inc.
3800 Hamlin Road
Auburn Hills, MI 48326
Phone: (810) 340-5000 Fax: (810) 340-5540

Volvo North America Corp.
535 Madison Ave.
New York, NY 10022
Phone: (212) 754-3300 Fax: (212) 418-7435

Automobile Resource Organizations

AAA- American Automobile Association
1712 G Street N.W.
Washington, D.C. 20006

U.S. Environmental Protection Agency
Field Operations and Support Division (6406J)
401 M. Street S.W.
Washington, D.C. 20460

California Air Resources Board
9528 Telstar Ave.
El Monte, CA 91731

American Automobile Association
1712 G Street, NW
Washington, DC 20006

Better Business Bureau
Provides reports on dealers and other consumer information, and operates the "AutoLine" arbitration service. BBB has about 180 offices nationwide; check the listing in your local phone book for the nearest location.

Center for Auto Safety
2001 S Street, NW
Suite 410
Washington, D.C. 20009
(202) 328-7700

A non-profit organization that lobbies on behalf of consumers in areas of vehicle safety and quality.

Environmental Protection Agency
401 M Street, SW
Washington, D.C. 20460
(202) 260-2090

The EPA's annual Gas Mileage Guide gives data on fuel economy; this agency also enforces emissions laws.

Federal Trade Commission
6th and Pennsylvania Avenues, NW
Washington, D.C.20580
(202) 326-2222

The FTC has information on consumer complaints, deceptive business practices and arbitration. It maintains regional offices in Atlanta, Boston, Chicago, Cleveland, Dallas, Denver, Los Angeles, New York, San Francisco and Seattle. Write or call the Public Reference Section of one of these offices for free fact sheets on "Buying a Used Car," "Vehicle Repossessions," "Warranties," or "Service Contracts". Contact the Division of Enforcement with complaints about window sticker violations; contact the Division of Marketing for warranty problems.

Highway Loss Data Institute/Insurance Institute for Highway Safety
1005 N. Glebe Road
Arlington, VA 22201
(703) 247-1500

Kelley Blue Book Used Car Guide
P. O. Box 19691
Irvine, CA 92713
(800) BLUE BOOK/(800) 258-3266/(714) 770-7704/FAX: (714) 837-1904

The Kelley Blue Book is a bimonthly publication which provides information such as list prices, wholesale values, suggested retail values, optional equipment schedules, mileage adjustment schedules, etc. for used cars. You can usually find the Kelley Blue Book at your local library.

NADA Appraisal Guides
P.O. Box 7800
Costa Mesa, CA 92628-9924
(800) 966-6232/(714) 556-8511

NADA (National Automobile Dealers Association) puts out a large line of monthly to quarterly appraisal guides for used cars, commercial trucks, RVs, motorcycles, etc. NADA books contain information similar to Kelley's, but it's always good to get a second opinion. Like Kelley Blue Books, NADA Guides should be available in your local library.

National Highway Traffic Safety Administration
400 Seventh Street, SW
Washington, D.C. 20590
Consumer hotline: 1-800-424-9393
Hearing-impaired people: 1-800-424-9153

The NHTSA provides brochures on odometer fraud, tire grades, safety belts and air bags, child safety seats, safety standards, new-car crash test results and safety recalls.

Owner's manuals

Automotive Information Clearinghouse
P.O. Box 1746
LaMesa, CA 92044
(619) 447-7200
AIC sells used owner's manuals for most makes and models.

Dyment Distribution Services
Service Publications
P.O. Box 360450
Strongsville, OH 44136
(216) 572-7240/FAX: (216) 572-0815
Dyment distributes new owner's manuals manuals for Chrysler/Jeep/Eagle and Nissan products.

Faxon Auto Literature
1655 East 6th Street
Corona, CA 91719
(800) 458-2734
Faxon sells used and new-reprinted owner's manuals for most makes and models.

Helm, Inc.
(800) 782-4356
Helm distributes new owner's manuals manuals for Acura/Honda, Ford (Ford, Lincoln and Mercury), GM (Buick, Cadillac, Chevrolet, Geo, GMC, Oldsmobile and Pontiac), Isuzu, Kia and Mazda products.

Toyota Service Publications
(800) 443-7656 (West coast)
(800) 662-2033 (East coast)
Toyota owner's manuals.

Helpful books

Consumer Guide Used Car Book, new edition every year, Publications International Ltd. This book contains profiles of all the popular makes and models and includes such information as price ranges, major safety recalls, frequent mechanical problems, fuel economy estimates, key specifications, shopping advice and best bets.

The Insider's Guide to Buying a New or Used Car, by Burke and Stephanie Leon; 1993, Betterway Books, Cincinnati, Ohio. Light on technical information but authoritatively written by someone well acquainted with the paperwork of buying a car - getting loans, trade-ins, calculating dealer costs, financing, etc. But the best parts of this book are the sections dealing with the psychology of buying a used car - dealer tactics, buyer tactics, negotiating, etc.

The Used Car Reliability and Safety Guide, by Adam Berliant; 1994, Betterway Books, Cincinnati, Ohio. This 360-page large-format paperback lists popular vehicles by make and model. Under each entry, the author has included an accident rating, a recall alert and trouble spots on the vehicle. The data was compiled from National Highway Traffic Safety Administration (NHTSA) figures. A handy guide for eliminating obvious losers from consideration.

Used Car Buying Guide, by the editors of Consumer Reports Books; new edition every year, Consumer Reports Books, a division of Consumers Union, Yonkers, N.Y. This book is a gold mine of information about late-model used cars. The book includes a wide and relevant collection of offprints from road tests of popular makes and models that originally appeared in Consumers Report magazine, where each tested vehicle was rated for handling, fuel economy, ride quality, noise levels, acceleration, braking, emergency handling, driving position, seating, safety, controls and displays, trunk, cargo area, climate system, etc. Also included are frequency-of-repair charts for hundreds of models, a list of cars to avoid, and recalls of autos, trucks, minivans and sport-utility vehicles. You may also want to consult back issues of the annual automobile issue of the monthly Consumer Reports magazine. They'll give you a lot of essential background information about any model.

Appendix D
Preparing for emissions certification testing

Over half of all states now require regular - annual or biannual - emission certification tests. Many also require smog inspections when vehicle ownership changes hands. Often the seller will assume the responsibility of the smog inspection; this is certainly the case when buying a car from a car lot. But if the responsibility is yours and if someone has "modified" (tampered with) the vehicle's smog equipment, this ritual of having the vehicle "smogged" can give you an anxiety attack. And even if you're the type of owner who would never dream of disconnecting a single vacuum line the previous owner, or owners, may have tampered with the emissions system in such a way as to cause the vehicle to fail the state smog inspection. Recent statistics from some states indicate that nearly one-third of all vehicles fail to meet emissions standards their first time through.

With a straight-forward check of emissions-related components, you can catch nearly all the potential failures which might turn up in a state inspection. And you might as well get used to it, because state-certified smog testing is going to become stricter and more frequent as time goes on. Specific testing procedures and standards for various emissions levels vary from state to state, but the idea - lowering the HC, CO and NOx levels - is the same everywhere. So the following information should save you time and money. Time because you won't have to go back several times to pass the test; money because you won't have to shell out extra dollars for the repairs needed to enable your vehicle to pass the test.

Generally, a stock (untampered with) engine will pass the state smog test as long as it's been recently tuned and all the emissions-related hardware is intact, hooked up and working properly. If your vehicle hasn't had a tune-up recently, now is the time to do it.

The following items should be checked carefully before a smog test:

1) Make a quick visual check of all emissions control systems to be sure all components are in place and hooked up correctly. If you have reason to suspect a system is not functioning correctly, check it, as described in Chapter 3.
2) Inspect all underhood vacuum hoses for cracks, loose connections and disconnected hoses.
3) Inspect all underhood electrical wiring for cracks, torn wires, loose or corroded connections and unplugged connectors.
4) Check the air filter carefully, since a dirty, restricted air filter will cause a rich fuel/air mixture, increasing emissions. Also check the PCV filter, if equipped (see Chapter 3).
5) On carbureted models, check the choke to be sure it's opening all the way when the engine is warmed up (here again, the rich fuel/air mixture caused by a closed choke will increase emissions).
6) Finally, before having vehicle car tested, make sure the engine and exhaust (catalytic converter) system are up to normal temperature (10 to 15 minutes of driving time).

How do you pick a shop for an emissions test?

Where do you take your vehicle for a smog test? Well, if you already have a good working relationship with a local shop - and it's certified to do smog testing - by all means stick with that shop. But if you don't have a regular shop, there are several factors worth considering: First, look at what the shop charges. This isn't as important as you might think; the inspection fees charged by private garages are generally regulated by the state, so there may not be that much difference in fees from one shop to another. The important thing to keep in mind is that the fee charged by most shops is usually a lot lower than its normal hourly labor rate. In other words, doing emissions testing can be a marginally profitable - or even a losing proposition - for shops. So how does a shop turn a smog test into a money maker? Basically, by charging you their normal labor rate for fixing problems if your vehicle fails its smog test.

Of course, you're certainly not obligated to have your vehicle repaired by the same shop that inspects it for compliance with state smog laws. But the shop owner hopes you will do just that, to avoid the inconvenience of moving the vehicle to another shop. Whether you decide to have the vehicle repaired by the same shop that inspects it, or take it somewhere else, depends on how much you trust the shop's ethics.

Also, try to find a shop that does not charge for re-testing your vehicle if it should fail the test. Re-testing fees - particularly if your vehicle must be re-tested more than once - can really add up.

The emissions test

Most state smog certification inspections consist of two parts:

1) An under-hood visual inspection - to make sure everything is installed and connected.
2) An analysis of the composition of the exhaust gases coming out the tailpipe, both at idle and at median on-the-road engine speeds.

You might survive the first part of the test even if something is missing or everything isn't hooked up, because the mechanic may or may not be familiar with the emissions devices and systems that are supposed to be fitted to your engine. But don't bet on it. The software programs employed by most state-approved emissions-testing analyzers display this information - component identification and location of all emission components for your specific model - on the video screen of the analyzer.

But even if your vehicle passes the visual inspection phase in spite of a missing or disconnected device or system, the engine will probably fail the second part of the test, which is performed with an infrared gas analyzer.

A probe, which is shoved up the tailpipe, detects the amount of hydrocarbons (HC), carbon monoxide (CO) and oxides of nitrogen (NOx) in the exhaust stream, and transmits this information to a computer which measures these levels to a high degree of accuracy (expressed in "parts per million," or ppm). This analysis of the exhaust gases is usually conducted both at idle speed and at about 2500 to 2800 rpm. If the engine fails either part, the vehicle fails the test.

The analyzer computer prints out two hard copies of the HC and CO readings, one for you and one for the shop's inspection records. How do you know whether the analyzer's conclusions are accurate? Most analyzers are self-calibrating: Every time they're turned on to perform a test, they verify the validity of their calibration against reference gases contained inside their own apparatus. If your vehicle passes its emissions test, you're allowed to drive it for another year or two. If it fails, you have a "grace period," usually a month, to bring the vehicle up to specification so that it can pass (unless, of course, you have waited until the last minute to submit your vehicle to the test and your registration is about to expire, in which case you have considerably less time to fix it!).

What if your vehicle fails the emissions test?

If your vehicle fails its emissions test, see the information in *Warranties* found in Chapter 1.

Appendix E
Preparing for a safety inspection

Safety should be a top concern to every car owner and driver. Many states have required safety inspections which all resident vehicles must pass prior to or concurrently with registration. Obviously, it is not possible for you to check the car to the same standard as a professional state tester, who will be highly experienced and will have all the necessary tools and equipment, but the following should provide you with a good indication as to the general condition of the car and will enable you to identify any obvious problem areas before submitting your car for the test. This section is intended as a general overview only. For more complete maintenance of safety-related components, please refer to the *Haynes Automotive Repair Manual* for your particular car or truck.

Lights

All lights must work, and the lenses and reflectors must not be damaged. Pairs of similar lights must be of the same brightness (e.g. both rear lights). Both headlights must show the same color and must be correctly aimed so that they light up the road adequately but don't dazzle other drivers. Headlight aiming should normally be performed by a professional; however, temporary adjustments can be carried out using the procedure in the *Haynes Automotive Electrical Manual*.

Both brake lights must work when the brake pedal is pressed, and the lights must come on before or concurrently with braking action.

The turn signal lights should flash between one and two times per second.

Steering and suspension

All the components and their mounting points should be secure. Be sure there is no damage or excessive corrosion.

There should be no excessive freeplay in the joints and bushings. Also, check that all rubber dust boots are secure and undamaged.

The steering mechanism should operate smoothly without excessive freeplay or roughness.

There should be no excessive freeplay or roughness in the wheel bearings, but there should be sufficient ease of motion to prevent binding.

There should be no major fluid leaks from the shock absorbers and, when each corner of the car is pressed down, it should rise and then settle into its normal position (bouncing indicates a shock absorber failure).

The driveshaft (on rear wheel drive cars) should not be damaged or distorted.

Brakes

It should be possible to operate the parking brake without excessive force or excessive movement of the lever, and it should not be possible for the lever to release unintentionally. The parking brake must be able to lock the rear wheels (or front wheels on some Subarus and Saabs). A good test for the parking brake is to park the vehicle on the steepest hill you can find and apply the parking brake securely. If the brake can hold on a steep hill, it's probably OK.

The brake pedal should not be damaged or excessively worn, and, when the pedal is pressed, resistance should be felt near the top of its travel - hard resistance should be felt (no "spongy" feel) and the pedal should hold the same height under hard pedal pressure for 30 seconds (it should not sink any further towards the floor under constant pressure).

There should be no signs of any fluid leaks anywhere in the braking system. The wheels should turn freely when the brakes are not applied.

When the brakes are applied, the brakes on all four wheels must work, and the car should stop evenly in a straight line without pulling to one side.

All the braking system components should be secure and show no signs of excessive wear or corrosion. Pay particular attention to the friction linings on the brake pads and/or shoes, which should have at least 20-percent of their original (new) thickness.

Tires and wheels

The tires should be in good condition and inflated to the vehicle manufacturer's specification, which is in the owner's manual and stamped onto the Safety Certification Label (usually attached to the driver's door jamb).

The treads must be at least 1/32" thick. You may check tread thickness with a thickness gauge, or you may take a penny from your pocket and place the top of President Lincoln's head into the most worn area of each tire. If the top edge of Mr. Lincoln's head remains visible while resting in the tread, you'll need to replace the tire.

Tires at the same end of the car must be of the same size and type.

Tires should not show signs of abnormal wear

Seatbelts

The mountings must be secure and must not be loose or excessively corroded. The seatbelt fabric should not be frayed or torn (this must be checked along the full length of the belt).

When a seatbelt is fastened, the locking mechanism should hold securely and should release when intended.

In the case of inertia-reel seatbelts, the retractors should work properly when the belts are released.

Electronic automatic seatbelts on some 1990 and later vehicles must function as originally designed.

Exhaust system

The exhaust system should be in good condition and route exhaust to the rear of the vehicle. Most cars and light trucks should have the exhaust exiting behind the rear wheels.

There should be no rust-through or other holes anywhere in the exhaust system (pipes, muffler, resonator or catalytic converter). Small holes can be repaired by welding or using an approved exhaust system sealer, but large holes will require component replacement.

A technique that may help when checking for exhaust system leaks is to, while the engine is running, momentarily stuff a rag into the tailpipe(s) and look/feel for exhaust leaks at component flanges and pipe joints. **Warning 1:** *Don't touch exhaust system components during this check, or you could severely burn yourself! Hold your hand slightly away from the components - the back-pressure created by the rag in the tailpipe will cause leaks to be strongly pressurized.* **Warning 2:** *Never place any part of your body under a running car unless it is safely supported - a service station with a lift is the only truly safe place to carry out this check.* **Caution:** *Don't leave the rag in the tailpipe for more than a few seconds at a time or engine damage could result!*

General

Take a look under the hood to see that all system hoses are in good shape. They should all be properly connected and should show no signs of cracking or leakage.

Check that all drivebelts are taught and that they are not cracked or frayed.

It's a good idea while you're looking at the engine area to make sure that all components seem to be attached the way they were intended to (e.g. no loose or rattling parts, no exhaust pipes held up by hanger wire, no funky "custom" wiring jobs, etc.).

The windshield must be crack-free, and the windshield wipers and washers must work properly. The wiper blades must clear the windshield without smearing.

The horn must work properly.

The exhaust mountings must be secure, and the system itself must be free from leaks and serious corrosion.

There must be no serious corrosion or damage to the vehicle structure. Corrosion of body panels will not necessarily cause a car to fail the test, but there should be no serious corrosion of any of the load-bearing structural components. The fenders should still surround the top halves of the wheels and have no large holes.

The exhaust gas emissions level must be within certain limits, depending on the age of the car (special equipment is required to measure exhaust gas emissions). Also, check visually for excessive exhaust smoke out the tailpipe. Generally speaking, the car should meet emissions regulations if regular servicing has been carried out and the engine is running well.

Index

The Haynes Used Car Buying Guide

HAYNES AUTOMOTIVE MANUALS

ACURA
*1776 **Integra & Legend** all models '86 thru '90

AMC
Jeep CJ - see JEEP (412)
694 **Mid-size models,** Concord, Hornet, Gremlin & Spirit '70 thru '83
934 **(Renault) Alliance & Encore** all models '83 thru '87

AUDI
615 **4000** all models '80 thru '87
428 **5000** all models '77 thru '83
1117 **5000** all models '84 thru '88

AUSTIN
Healey Sprite - see MG Midget Roadster (265)

BMW
*2020 **3/5 Series** not including diesel or all-wheel drive models '82 thru '92
276 **320i** all 4 cyl models '75 thru '83
632 **528i & 530i** all models '75 thru '80
240 **1500 thru 2002** all models except Turbo '59 thru '77
348 **2500, 2800, 3.0 & Bavaria** all models '69 thru '76

BUICK
Century (front wheel drive) - see GENERAL MOTORS (829)
*1627 **Buick, Oldsmobile & Pontiac Full-size (Front wheel drive)** all models '85 thru '93
Buick Electra, LeSabre and Park Avenue; Oldsmobile Delta 88 Royale, Ninety Eight and Regency; Pontiac Bonneville
1551 **Buick Oldsmobile & Pontiac Full-size (Rear wheel drive)**
Buick Estate '70 thru '90, Electra'70 thru '84, LeSabre '70 thru '85, Limited '74 thru '79
Oldsmobile Custom Cruiser '70 thru '90, Delta 88 '70 thru '85,Ninety-eight '70 thru '84
Pontiac Bonneville '70 thru '81, Catalina '70 thru '81, Grandville '70 thru '75, Parisienne '83 thru '86
627 **Mid-size Regal & Century** all rear-drive models with V6, V8 and Turbo '74 thru '87
Regal - see GENERAL MOTORS (1671)
Skyhawk - see GENERAL MOTORS (766)
552 **Skylark** all X-car models '80 thru '85
Skylark '86 on - see GENERAL MOTORS (1420)
Somerset - see GENERAL MOTORS (1420)

CADILLAC
*751 **Cadillac Rear Wheel Drive** all gasoline models '70 thru '92
Cimarron - see GENERAL MOTORS (766)

CAPRI
296 **2000 MK I Coupe** all models '71 thru '75
Mercury Capri - see FORD Mustang (654)

CHEVROLET
*1477 **Astro & GMC Safari Mini-vans** '85 thru '93
554 **Camaro V8** all models '70 thru '81
866 **Camaro** all models '82 thru '92
Cavalier - see GENERAL MOTORS (766)
Celebrity - see GENERAL MOTORS (829)
625 **Chevelle, Malibu & El Camino** all V6 & V8 models '69 thru '87
449 **Chevette & Pontiac T1000** '76 thru '87
550 **Citation** all models '80 thru '85

*1628 **Corsica/Beretta** all models '87 thru '92
274 **Corvette** all V8 models '68 thru '82
*1336 **Corvette** all models '84 thru '91
1762 **Chevrolet Engine Overhaul Manual**
704 **Full-size Sedans** Caprice, Impala, Biscayne, Bel Air & Wagons '69 thru '90
Lumina - see GENERAL MOTORS (1671)
Lumina APV - see GENERAL MOTORS (2035)
319 **Luv Pick-up** all 2WD & 4WD '72 thru '82
626 **Monte Carlo** all models '70 thru '88
241 **Nova** all V8 models '69 thru '79
*1642 **Nova and Geo Prizm** all front wheel drive models, '85 thru '92
420 **Pick-ups '67 thru '87** - Chevrolet & GMC, all V8 & in-line 6 cyl, 2WD & 4WD '67 thru '87; Suburbans, Blazers & Jimmys '67 thru '91
*1664 **Pick-ups '88 thru '93** - Chevrolet & GMC, all full-size (C and K) models, '88 thru '93
*831 **S-10 & GMC S-15 Pick-ups** all models '82 thru '92
*1727 **Sprint & Geo Metro** '85 thru '91
*345 **Vans - Chevrolet & GMC,** V8 & in-line 6 cylinder models '68 thru '92

CHRYSLER
*2058 **Full-size Front-Wheel Drive** '88 thru '93
K-Cars - see DODGE Aries (723)
Laser - see DODGE Daytona (1140)
*1337 **Chrysler & Plymouth Mid-size** front wheel drive '82 thru '93

DATSUN
402 **200SX** all models '77 thru '79
647 **200SX** all models '80 thru '83
228 **B - 210** all models '73 thru '78
525 **210** all models '78 thru '82
206 **240Z, 260Z & 280Z** Coupe '70 thru '78
563 **280ZX** Coupe & 2+2 '79 thru '83
300ZX - see NISSAN (1137)
679 **310** all models '78 thru '82
123 **510 & PL521 Pick-up** '68 thru '73
430 **510** all models '78 thru '81
372 **610** all models '72 thru '76
277 **620 Series Pick-up** all models '73 thru '79
720 Series Pick-up - see NISSAN (771)
376 **810/Maxima** all gasoline models, '77 thru '84
368 **F10** all models '76 thru '79
Pulsar - see NISSAN (876)
Sentra - see NISSAN (982)
Stanza - see NISSAN (981)

DODGE
400 & 600 - see CHRYSLER Mid-size (1337)
*723 **Aries & Plymouth Reliant** '81 thru '89
*1231 **Caravan & Plymouth Voyager Mini-Vans** all models '84 thru '93
699 **Challenger & Plymouth Saporro** all models '78 thru '83
Challenger '67-'76 - see DODGE Dart (234)
236 **Colt** all models '71 thru '77
610 **Colt & Plymouth Champ (front wheel drive)** all models '78 thru '87
*1668 **Dakota Pick-ups** all models '87 thru '93
234 **Dart, Challenger/Plymouth Barracuda & Valiant** 6 cyl models '67 thru '76
*1140 **Daytona & Chrysler Laser** '84 thru '89
*545 **Omni & Plymouth Horizon** '78 thru '90
*912 **Pick-ups** all full-size models '74 thru '91
*556 **Ram 50/D50 Pick-ups & Raider and Plymouth Arrow Pick-ups** '79 thru '93
*1726 **Shadow & Plymouth Sundance** '87 thru '93
*1779 **Spirit & Plymouth Acclaim** '89 thru '92
*349 **Vans - Dodge & Plymouth** V8 & 6 cyl models '71 thru '91

EAGLE
Talon - see Mitsubishi Eclipse (2097)

FIAT
094 **124 Sport Coupe & Spider** '68 thru '78
273 **X1/9** all models '74 thru '80

FORD
*1476 **Aerostar Mini-vans** all models '86 thru '92
788 **Bronco and Pick-ups** '73 thru '79
*880 **Bronco and Pick-ups** '80 thru '91
268 **Courier Pick-up** all models '72 thru '82
1763 **Ford Engine Overhaul Manual**
789 **Escort/Mercury Lynx** all models '81 thru '90
*2046 **Escort/Mercury Tracer** '91 thru '93
*2021 **Explorer & Mazda Navajo** '91 thru '92
560 **Fairmont & Mercury Zephyr** '78 thru '83
334 **Fiesta** all models '77 thru '80
754 **Ford & Mercury Full-size,** Ford LTD & Mercury Marquis ('75 thru '82); Ford Custom 500,Country Squire, Crown Victoria & Mercury Colony Park ('75 thru '87); Ford LTD Crown Victoria & Mercury Gran Marquis ('83 thru '87)
359 **Granada & Mercury Monarch** all in-line, 6 cyl & V8 models '75 thru '80
773 **Ford & Mercury Mid-size,** Ford Thunderbird & Mercury Cougar ('75 thru '82); Ford LTD & Mercury Marquis ('83 thru '86); Ford Torino,Gran Torino, Elite, Ranchero pick-up, LTD II, Mercury Montego, Comet, XR-7 & Lincoln Versailles ('75 thru '86)
*654 **Mustang & Mercury Capri** all models including Turbo. Mustang, '79 thru '92; Capri, '79 thru '86
357 **Mustang V8** all models '64-1/2 thru '73
231 **Mustang II** 4 cyl, V6 & V8 models '74 thru '78
649 **Pinto & Mercury Bobcat** '75 thru '80
1670 **Probe** all models '89 thru '92
*1026 **Ranger/Bronco II** gasoline models '83 thru '93
*1421 **Taurus & Mercury Sable** '86 thru '92
*1418 **Tempo & Mercury Topaz** all gasoline models '84 thru '93
1338 **Thunderbird/Mercury Cougar** '83 thru '88
*1725 **Thunderbird/Mercury Cougar** '89 and '90
*344 **Vans** all V8 Econoline models '69 thru '91

GENERAL MOTORS
*829 **Buick Century, Chevrolet Celebrity, Oldsmobile Cutlass Ciera & Pontiac 6000** all models '82 thru '93
*766 **Buick Skyhawk, Cadillac Cimarron, Chevrolet Cavalier, Oldsmobile Firenza & Pontiac J-2000 & Sunbird** all models '82 thru '92
1420 **Buick Skylark & Somerset, Oldsmobile Calais & Pontiac Grand Am** all models '85 thru '91
*1671 **Buick Regal, Chevrolet Lumina, Oldsmobile Cutlass Supreme & Pontiac Grand Prix** all front wheel drive models '88 thru '90
*2035 **Chevrolet Lumina APV, Oldsmobile Silhouette & Pontiac Trans Sport** all models '90 thru '92

GEO
Metro - see CHEVROLET Sprint (1727)
Prizm - see CHEVROLET Nova (1642)
*2039 **Storm** all models '90 thru '93
Tracker - see SUZUKI Samurai (1626)

GMC
Safari - see CHEVROLET ASTRO (1477)
Vans & Pick-ups - see CHEVROLET (420, 831, 345, 1664)

(Continued on other side)

Haynes North America, Inc., 861 Lawrence Drive, Newbury Park, CA 91320 • (805) 498-6703

HAYNES AUTOMOTIVE MANUALS

NOTE: New manuals are added to this list on a periodic basis. If you do not see a listing for your vehicle, consult your local Haynes dealer for the latest product information.

HONDA

351	Accord CVCC all models '76 thru '83
1221	Accord all models '84 thru '89
2067	Accord all models '90 thru '93
160	Civic 1200 all models '73 thru '79
633	Civic 1300 & 1500 CVCC '80 thru '83
297	Civic 1500 CVCC all models '75 thru '79
1227	Civic all models '84 thru '91
*601	Prelude CVCC all models '79 thru '89

HYUNDAI

*1552	Excel all models '86 thru '93

ISUZU

*1641	Trooper & Pick-up, all gasoline models Pick-up, '81 thru '93; Trooper, '84 thru '91

JAGUAR

*242	XJ6 all 6 cyl models '68 thru '86
*478	XJ12 & XJS all 12 cyl models '72 thru '85

JEEP

*1553	Cherokee, Comanche & Wagoneer Limited all models '84 thru '93
412	CJ all models '49 thru '86
*1777	Wrangler all models '87 thru '92

LADA

*413	1200, 1300. 1500 & 1600 all models including Riva '74 thru '91

MAZDA

648	626 Sedan & Coupe (rear wheel drive) all models '79 thru '82
*1082	626 & MX-6 (front wheel drive) all models '83 thru '91
267	B Series Pick-ups '72 thru '93
370	GLC Hatchback (rear wheel drive) all models '77 thru '83
757	GLC (front wheel drive) '81 thru '85
*2047	MPV all models '89 thru '93
460	RX-7 all models '79 thru '85
*1419	RX-7 all models '86 thru '91

MERCEDES-BENZ

*1643	190 Series all four-cylinder gasoline models '84 thru '88
346	230, 250 & 280 Sedan, Coupe & Roadster all 6 cyl sohc models '68 thru '72
983	280 123 Series gasoline models '77 thru '81
698	350 & 450 Sedan, Coupe & Roadster all models '71 thru '80
697	Diesel 123 Series 200D, 220D, 240D, 240TD, 300D, 300CD, 300TD, 4- & 5-cyl incl. Turbo '76 thru '85

MERCURY

See FORD Listing

MG

111	MGB Roadster & GT Coupe all models '62 thru '80
265	MG Midget & Austin Healey Sprite Roadster '58 thru '80

MITSUBISHI

*1669	Cordia, Tredia, Galant, Precis & Mirage '83 thru '93
*2022	Pick-up & Montero '83 thru '93
*2097	Eclipse, Eagle Talon & Plymouth Laser '90 thru '94

MORRIS

074	(Austin) Marina 1.8 all models '71 thru '78
024	Minor 1000 sedan & wagon '56 thru '71

NISSAN

1137	300ZX all models including Turbo '84 thru '89
*1341	Maxima all models '85 thru '91
*771	Pick-ups/Pathfinder gas models '80 thru '93
876	Pulsar all models '83 thru '86
*982	Sentra all models '82 thru '90
*981	Stanza all models '82 thru '90

OLDSMOBILE

	Bravada - see CHEVROLET S-10 (831)
	Calais - see GENERAL MOTORS (1420)
	Custom Cruiser - see BUICK Full-size RWD (1551)
*658	Cutlass all standard gasoline V6 & V8 models '74 thru '88
	Cutlass Ciera - see GENERAL MOTORS (829)
	Cutlass Supreme - see GM (1671)
	Delta 88 - see BUICK Full-size RWD (1551)
	Delta 88 Brougham - see BUICK Full-size FWD (1551), RWD (1627)
	Delta 88 Royale - see BUICK Full-size RWD (1551)
	Firenza - see GENERAL MOTORS (766)
	Ninety-eight Regency - see BUICK Full-size RWD (1551), FWD (1627)
	Ninety-eight Regency Brougham - see BUICK Full-size RWD (1551)
	Omega - see PONTIAC Phoenix (551)
	Silhouette - see GENERAL MOTORS (2035)

PEUGEOT

663	504 all diesel models '74 thru '83

PLYMOUTH

	Laser - see MITSUBISHI Eclipse (2097)
	For other PLYMOUTH titles, see DODGE listing.

PONTIAC

	T1000 - see CHEVROLET Chevette (449)
	J-2000 - see GENERAL MOTORS (766)
	6000 - see GENERAL MOTORS (829)
	Bonneville - see Buick Full-size FWD (1627), RWD (1551)
	Bonneville Brougham - see Buick Full-size (1551)
	Catalina - see Buick Full-size (1551)
1232	Fiero all models '84 thru '88
555	Firebird V8 models except Turbo '70 thru '81
867	Firebird all models '82 thru '92
	Full-size Rear Wheel Drive - see BUICK Oldsmobile, Pontiac Full-size RWD (1551)
	Full-size Front Wheel Drive - see BUICK Oldsmobile, Pontiac Full-size FWD (1627)
	Grand Am - see GENERAL MOTORS (1420)
	Grand Prix - see GENERAL MOTORS (1671)
	Grandville - see BUICK Full-size (1551)
	Parisienne - see BUICK Full-size (1551)
551	Phoenix & Oldsmobile Omega all X-car models '80 thru '84
	Sunbird - see GENERAL MOTORS (766)
	Trans Sport - see GENERAL MOTORS (2035)

PORSCHE

*264	911 all Coupe & Targa models except Turbo & Carrera 4 '65 thru '89
239	914 all 4 cyl models '69 thru '76
397	924 all models including Turbo '76 thru '82
*1027	944 all models including Turbo '83 thru '89

RENAULT

141	5 Le Car all models '76 thru '83
079	8 & 10 58.4 cu in engines '62 thru '72
097	12 Saloon & Estate 1289 cc engine '70 thru '80
768	15 & 17 all models '73 thru '79
081	16 89.7 cu in & 95.5 cu in engines '65 thru '72
	Alliance & Encore - see AMC (934)

SAAB

247	99 all models including Turbo '69 thru '80
*980	900 all models including Turbo '79 thru '88

SUBARU

237	1100, 1300, 1400 & 1600 '71 thru '79
*681	1600 & 1800 2WD & 4WD '80 thru '89

SUZUKI

*1626	Samurai/Sidekick and Geo Tracker all models '86 thru '93

TOYOTA

1023	Camry all models '83 thru '91
150	Carina Sedan all models '71 thru '74
935	Celica Rear Wheel Drive '71 thru '85
*2038	Celica Front Wheel Drive '86 thru '92
1139	Celica Supra all models '79 thru '92
361	Corolla all models '75 thru '79
961	Corolla all rear wheel drive models '80 thru '87
*1025	Corolla all front wheel drive models '84 thru '92
636	Corolla Tercel all models '80 thru '82
360	Corona all models '74 thru '82
532	Cressida all models '78 thru '82
313	Land Cruiser all models '68 thru '82
200	MK II all 6 cyl models '72 thru '76
*1339	MR2 all models '85 thru '87
304	Pick-up all models '69 thru '78
*656	Pick-up all models '79 thru '92
*2048	Previa all models '91 thru '93

TRIUMPH

112	GT6 & Vitesse all models '62 thru '74
113	Spitfire all models '62 thru '81
322	TR7 all models '75 thru '81

VW

159	Beetle & Karmann Ghia all models '54 thru '79
238	Dasher all gasoline models '74 thru '81
*884	Rabbit, Jetta, Scirocco, & Pick-up gas models '74 thru '91 & Convertible '80 thru '92
451	Rabbit, Jetta & Pick-up all diesel models '77 thru '84
082	Transporter 1600 all models '68 thru '79
226	Transporter 1700, 1800 & 2000 all models '72 thru '79
084	Type 3 1500 & 1600 all models '63 thru '73
1029	Vanagon all air-cooled models '80 thru '83

VOLVO

203	120, 130 Series & 1800 Sports '61 thru '73
129	140 Series all models '66 thru '74
*270	240 Series all models '74 thru '90
400	260 Series all models '75 thru '82
*1550	740 & 760 Series all models '82 thru '88

SPECIAL MANUALS

1479	Automotive Body Repair & Painting Manual
1654	Automotive Electrical Manual
1667	Automotive Emissions Control Manual
1480	Automotive Heating & Air Conditioning Manual
1762	Chevrolet Engine Overhaul Manual
1736	GM and Ford Diesel Engine Repair Manual
1763	Ford Engine Overhaul Manual
482	Fuel Injection Manual
2069	Holley Carburetor Manual
1666	Small Engine Repair Manual
299	SU Carburetors thru '88
393	Weber Carburetors thru '79
300	Zenith/Stromberg CD Carburetors thru '76

Over 100 Haynes motorcycle manuals also available

* Listings shown with an asterisk (*) indicate model coverage as of this printing. These titles will be periodically updated to include later model years - consult your Haynes dealer for more information.

Haynes North America, Inc., 861 Lawrence Drive, Newbury Park, CA 91320 • (805) 498-6703